In Pursuit of the
Christ-Shaped Life

In Pursuit of the Christ-Shaped Life

Philippians on Christian Formation

MICAH D. CARPENTER

WIPF & STOCK · Eugene, Oregon

IN PURSUIT OF THE CHRIST-SHAPED LIFE
Phillipians on Christian Formation

Wipf & Stock
An Imprint of Wipf and Stock Publishers
199 W. 8th Ave., Suite 3
Eugene, OR 97401

www.wipfandstock.com

PAPERBACK ISBN: 978-1-6667-1177-6
HARDCOVER ISBN: 978-1-6667-1178-3
EBOOK ISBN: 978-1-6667-1179-0

AUGUST 18, 2021

All scripture quotations, besides those provided by the author, are from the
New International Version (Grand Rapids, MI: Zondervan, 2011).

This book is dedicated to the many good friends and ministry partners I have found through my work with CIM (Center for Indian Ministries): Mark, Paul, Sam, Hannah, Barb, Nate, and many others. You are all Christ-shaped servants of God who have had a shaping influence in my life through your example of dedicated service.

Contents

Acknowledgements

IN THE WRITING OF any book, there are probably more people who deserve credit than who ever receive it. That is true partly because a book is the product of a person who has been shaped and influenced by more people than could be named. In my own case, there are countless people who have contributed to my Christian formation, and who have therefore played some role in the shaping of this book.

I am also indebted to many thinkers and authors who came before me. I have not laden my text with many footnotes, because this is a book of personal reflection rather than of academic study. But that does not mean that there are no influences behind my writing. In this particular book, I believe I am especially indebted to the thinking and writing of Augustine and C. S. Lewis. (Not at all to attempt to put myself in such great company—Augustine and Lewis are both figures whose influence deserves to be felt by all Christians.)

I would particularly like to thank the handful of people who helped in the production of this book. These include those who read early versions to give me feedback and encouragement: Justin Burpo, Micah Wilkinson, Justin Domogalla, Matthew Carpenter, and Michael Gorman.

1

What Shape Is Your Life?

PERHAPS WE DON'T NORMALLY think of our lives as having a "shape." Then again, when we pause to reflect, we often use the language of shape when describing aspects of our lives. We admire those people who have what we might call a "well-rounded" life. In stories and novels, we describe characters as being either "round" or "flat" to communicate the complexity of their characterization, or lack thereof. We invoke the physical shapes of the world's geography when we describe our life experiences, such as mountain-top triumphs or valleys of discouragement and loss. We talk about whether we are in good or poor shape—perhaps most directly when describing our physical health and fitness, but sometimes also when describing other aspects of our wellbeing. ("I'm afraid Joe's been in pretty bad shape ever since his wife passed away.")

We might also talk about the shape of our lives in ways that are even more specific than this. We recognize that we have all been shaped as persons by our communities, our relationships, our work, our experiences, our habits, our commitments, and our own choices. We are all unique individuals, yet we tend to adopt a pattern of life which resembles that of the people we spend time with. Our lives are very specifically (although not irresistibly) shaped by the influences of our husbands and wives, our parents and children, our friends and enemies, our coworkers and colleagues, and perhaps even our favorite TV characters. We are all, in a sense, like statues being chiseled into a certain shape by the various influences in our lives.

While this process of personal development may usually be the most intense while we are young, we are never done being shaped for as long as we live. Perhaps that is even a workable definition for what it means to be alive. The only place where we are immune from the forces of action and reaction which animate the world is the grave. Until the day we die, we are continuously confronted with the questions, "What kind of a person have I become?" and "What kind of a person am I now becoming?" In these questions lie the peril and the wonder of human life.

So I ask again: what kind of shape are you in? What shape is your life?

One of the biggest shaping factors in our lives is that of our own sense of identity. Either explicitly or implicitly, we wrestle with the question "Who am I," and seek an answer within our basic understanding of reality and within the contexts of our daily life.

This means that our identity is not merely something that sits passively in the background of our lives. Our sense of identity is constantly being shaped, and in turn, this imagined sense-of-self is always shaping us. One of our most important responsibilities in life is to come to proper terms with our sense of identity.

What's more, we want our sense of identity to be formed in alignment with the truth. Perhaps this runs counter to many contemporary notions of inventing our own identity, or trying on different identities much as we might try on different sets of clothes. That philosophy of life might seem very appealing up front, but I believe that it leaves us profoundly unfulfilled. We are all in search of an answer to the question of who we really are, and even more importantly, who we are supposed to be. The only answers of value are those which are found outside of ourselves. The alternative, in the end, is to be alone in a meaningless universe. What if I gaze out into the vastness of the cosmos, hungry for a hint of meaning, only to find that I am merely looking into a mirror? If there are no answers, desires, and destinies beyond those found by looking within ourselves, then we are in truth profoundly alone.

No, we want—or at least we ought to want—to find out where we fit in this world, and then learn how to live in light of that knowledge. We could refer to this as the personal discipline of identity: the process of being purposefully shaped as a "self" in relation to ultimate reality.

Of course, we as Christians do not believe that this is something which we can accomplish by ourselves, on our own terms, or according to our own initiative. For a Christian, the discipline of identity means coming to terms with the purposes and actions of God in Christ which already define us. The journey of the Christian life is one of becoming in daily life that which we already are in Christ. In this way, our present perspectives, priorities, and activities are to be rooted in that which God has already accomplished, and they are to be ever drawn toward the future which he has promised.

More specifically, amid all the influences which shape us, Christians are called to be shaped into the likeness of him whose name and identity we bear. That is the soul of Paul's message to the Philippians. It is a letter which famously bubbles over with joy, yet contains a sense of urgency. Not all urgency, after all, is negative. Indeed, the joyous duty of delighting in Christ may be the most urgent one entrusted to us. We have been given the glorious task and promise of embracing the Christ-shaped life.

ABOUT THIS BOOK

There are a number of intentions and motivations which guided me in writing this book. Perhaps more than anything else, I wrote it because Paul's letter to the Philippians has been close to my heart for a very long time, and I wanted a chance to study it more deeply. There are few better ways to meditate on a wonderful message than to write about it at length! However, there are a number of ways in which I hope this book may also prove helpful to others.

The Urgent Need for Joy-Filled Sanctification

First, I believe that there is a crucial need in the church today to give attention to the matter of sanctification: our growth in holiness after the pattern of Jesus, or, as we might call it, *Christoformity*. As a pastor, one of my deepest convictions is that God desires his church to be formed into the image of her Savior, Jesus Christ, and that he has provided powerful—indeed, inexorable—means for accomplishing this through his word and his Holy Spirit. I have written this book in part out of this sense of pastoral calling. I hope that this book will be helpful, in however small a way, for the sanctification of God's church in the pattern of Jesus Christ.

Sanctification is not, as is too often assumed, a mere afterthought to salvation, but rather the fulfillment of what salvation is about. God has not saved us merely to spare us something dreadful, but even more importantly, to give us something wonderful: an eternal life together which is conformed to the perfect model of human existence, Jesus Christ. God has created us, and now redeemed us, for the purpose of being shaped after the likeness of Christ.

But this is no mere personal, individual fulfillment. Such Christ-shaped people are urgently needed in our churches and in our world. Unfortunately, there are many people in our churches who have been "good Christians" for years with respect to their theology and their conformity to the norms of cultural Christianity, but who are still spiritually immature. In suggesting this, my intent is not to point fingers of blame at anyone, and certainly not to promote any attitude of snobbish elitism which looks down on those whom we regard as spiritually inferior. The presence of such an attitude is itself another form of spiritually immaturity. (And, the reader should note, I have not written this book because I am in any sense a person of profound spiritual maturity. I am no seasoned expert in the practices of Christian holiness. I am simply a Christian who enjoys writing about the Bible.) The issue which concerns me is an all-too pervasive failure of discipleship in the church. We have too often failed as worshiping communities to take seriously the call to edify one another; to challenge one another; to grow deeper together into the gospel; to vigorously spur one another on toward Christlikeness; to become passionate collaborators in one another's sanctification.

The book of Philippians offers us good help here. Like I've already said, Paul's message is all about the urgent yet joyful task of embracing the Christ-shaped life together and persevering on a wonderful—though sometimes perilous—journey toward the realization of God's purposes in salvation.

The sense of joy which permeates Philippians is one of the reasons why it is so helpful in addressing the urgent matter of spiritual formation in the church. Terms like "spiritual formation" and "discipleship" perhaps sometimes scare us away because they suggest a life of dreary moralism, legalistic fussiness, and religious monotony. These are all sub-Christian ideas of what spiritual formation is about, and the message of Philippians is a warm shaft of light which handily dispels such illusions. Here in Paul's letter we see a vision for spiritual formation which is not at all about guilt trips, grindstones, and "trying harder." Our growth toward Christlikeness may indeed involve hard work and even suffering at times, but fundamentally, spiritual formation is the work of joyfully embracing an identity and destiny which Christ has already achieved for us. It is the work of unwrapping a gift which has already been given to us; of embodying an identity which is already ours in Christ. This changes our idea of spiritual formation from that of an arduous, guilt-ridden discipline, to a sense of joyfully living each day as the adventure of participating in the life of Jesus Christ into which we have already been drawn.[1]

There is a crucial distinction at work here between two basic approaches to life. One we could call a compulsive approach, and other a propulsive approach. If we approach life compulsively, we are on an anxious quest to achieve something or to prove ourselves.

1. Dietrich Bonhoeffer put it like this: "To be conformed to the image of Christ is not an ideal to be striven after. It is not as though we had to imitate him as well as we could. We cannot transform ourselves into his image; it is rather the form of Christ which seeks to be formed in us (Gal. 4.19), and to be manifested in us." *Cost of Discipleship*, 298.

It is as though we are trying to climb a high mountain, scraping our bruised bodies over miles of rocks in the hope of reaching the prize at the top. But a propulsive posture in life is almost the opposite. Here we are living on the strength of something which has already been achieved. We are propelled forward by the power of a great gift we've already been given. It's as though the prize on the mountaintop has already been given to us, and in fact, we have been graciously lifted to the top ourselves. We are then so nourished in happiness that we're ready to run up the next mountain just for the fun of it.

This is important because so often spiritual formation, discipleship, and sanctification are topics we secretly dread to hear about. We think, "Oh boy, here comes another guilt trip." Perhaps we think of spiritual formation as a kind Christian elitism. Those who practice the spiritual disciplines, or at least those who excel at them, seem like Olympic athletes to us. We admire them, and might enjoy watching them sometimes, but most of us have no serious aspirations to become like them. But there's a major misunderstanding at work in all of this. Spiritual formation is not in the least about "trying harder," sticking our noses to a religious grindstone so as to achieve some rare, elite status. Spiritual formation is really very ordinary. It simply grows out of a right relationship with God, and out of right beliefs about God. If we really believe—and truly know—that God is good, that he is present with us, that he loves us dearly, that he's not out to get us but really wants us to come to him and to flourish and be happy in our relationship with him and others, then the practices of spiritual formation are simply things we will want to do. We want to talk to and read about and meditate on a God who is like that. Why wouldn't we? My desire for this book is that it will present a vision of Christian formation in its intrinsic beauty, and above all, to draw attention to the all-surpassing beauty of the gospel, and indeed of God himself.

The Need for Theologically-Grounded Sanctification

Second, this book is intended not only to be devotional and forma-
tional, but also to be theological. The proper habitat for theology
is in the life of God's people—in the church, in their reading of
God's word, in their prayer life, in their relationships—in short,
in the relationship between God and his people. That is a fact far
too easily forgotten. This book, then, is a theological reading of
Philippians directed toward the enrichment of the Christian life.
All spiritual formation and devotional practice cannot properly be
anything but enacted insight into the deep truths of God which
he has been pleased to reveal to us. True devotion is theological,
and true theology is devotional. Our theology must be brought
close to home. It cannot be confined to the academy, nor even to
the pulpit, but must dwell in the believer's heart, for theology is, in
fact, nothing other than the word of God spoken to us, treasured
in our hearts, and spoken back to him in the form of worship, love,
and obedience.

This book is therefore written according to the conviction
that one of the best modes of theological practice is direct engagement with Scripture, brought into dialogue with the Christian life.
Theology is too often construed as the practice of developing intellectual theories about God, rather than direct engagement with
the activity of God in revealing himself to us and seeking a right
response from us in our life together. This is what theology ought
to be about, even as it will rightly employ much intellectual theory
as a means to this end.

For this reason, I have written this book in a conversational
format. Each chapter begins with a passage from Philippians (my
own translation).[2] That is, each chapter starts with a passage of

2. A note on my translations: I have studied Greek, but that does not make
me a translation expert. I encourage readers to make use of at least one other
Bible translation. It should also be noted that my approach in translating Philippians is closer to paraphrase than word-for-word translation. I hope that
these translations give a fresh and clarifying view of the text, but again, I urge
the reader to make use of a good translation in reading Philippians alongside
this book—preferably a more word-for-word translation, such as the ESV,

God's word to us, and each chapter ends with a prayer of some sort (a human word uttered back to God.) In between these utterances are words intended to draw us into deeper reflection on God's word to us. My desire is that they will lead to many more prayers—prayers spoken with the lips, as well as those prayers which are embodied in the actions of God's people.

In a previous book I wrote, called *A Scandalous People*, I explored Paul's message in Ephesians and focused on his presentation of the gospel as something larger than life; namely, the cosmic and eternal purpose of God to demonstrate his goodness, wisdom, and love by creating a people of faith who exist through union with Christ and who stand in contrast to the powers of evil in the world. [3] This is, I believe, the same gospel which Paul preaches in Philippians (and indeed in all his letters). But here in this book is a presentation of the message which I hope goes more directly to the believer's heart. Just as we have branches of science which examine the workings of nature in the smallest particles as well as in the intergalactic structures of the universe, so Paul preaches a gospel which plays in all places, from the cosmic battle between God and the powers of evil, to the yearnings of the human heart. This book, then, is a more personal exposition of the great vision of reality which is Paul's gospel; namely, the people of God as those who have been drawn into union with the cruciform love of the Triune God. If I may be so bold, I would suggest that the very purpose of the universe and the meaning of human life is participation in the community of trinitarian love which was manifested on the cross. Ephesians paints this truth across a broad canvas, whereas Philippians sketches it in the most personal detail. In short, while my previous book on Ephesians explains the way in which the scandalous people participate in the cosmic purposes of God, this book on Philippians is like a devotional field guide for enacting the scandal in the context of daily life with God and others.

I conclude this introduction with a warning: books are usually worth far less than the things they are about. For example, even

RSV, or NASB.

3. Carpenter, *Scandalous People*.

the best book about butterflies is not one tenth as wonderful as are butterflies themselves. How much more so with a book about God. We must never settle merely for books about God when we can have God himself. We could merely read about God and think about him, or we could talk to him directly. We could spend our time reading about the Bible, or we could simply read the Bible. This does not mean that all other books are worthless. But the writer and the readers of this book must both remember that these pages are indeed worth nothing if they do not play the purpose of directing people toward God himself, the glorious words he has spoken to us, and the amazing, Christ-shaped life he has given to us and in which he has invited us to partake.

2

Toward the Day of Completion
The Christ-Shaped Life as Future Destiny and Well-Ordered Desire

PHILIPPIANS 1:1–11

From Paul and Timothy, servants of Christ Jesus,
To all God's holy people in Christ who live in Philippi, and to all your pastoral leaders:
Grace and peace be to you from God the Father and the Lord Jesus Christ!
Whenever I think of you and pray for you, I rejoice in thanksgiving to God. I am grateful for your partnership in the gospel which we have shared from day one, and I am confident in your future: that on the day of Christ Jesus, God will bring to completion the good work which he began in you. I am justified in thinking this way about all of you, because you have held me firmly in your heart throughout all my trials for the gospel, as I have defended it, confirmed it, and now am

imprisoned for it. And the feeling is mutual: God knows that I long for you all with the affection of Christ Jesus.

So this is my prayer for you: that your love may increasingly abound in knowledge and wisdom, so as to be able to discern that which has true, superior value. Then you will be found blameless and true on the day of Christ, whose righteousness will come to fruition in and through you, to the glory and praise of God.

ON HAVING A DESTINY

WHAT DOES IT MEAN to have a destiny?

Destiny is a concept that grips our imaginations. It does so in a number of ways, not all of which are positive. To feel oneself to have a destiny can be either encouraging or demoralizing; honoring or demeaning; life-giving or life-squelching. We may embrace the notion of destiny because it seems to give a meaning to our life, or we may reject it because it seems to rob us of meaning. It is remarkable how a single word can arouse so many different reactions.

There are a number of factors which may influence how we respond to the idea of destiny. One is what we perceive our destiny to be. If, for example, we believe that our lives are on a trajectory of unstoppable greatness, the idea of destiny seems thrilling, perhaps even to the point of boiling over into an intoxicating megalomania. On the other hand, if we believe that we are fated to live a life of powerlessness, mediocrity, abuse, or addiction, destiny seems like a demonically cruel curse.

Our response to the idea of destiny may also depend in part on how we interpret the meaning of the idea itself. If destiny means fate, a squelching determinism which abolishes our personal choice or responsibility, it is an idea which corrodes our sense of self, personhood, and meaning in life. If it is construed as a monolithic, supreme inevitability, it robs life of its drama and persons of their humanity.

But what if destiny means something different? What if it is not a river which pulls us along despite our struggles, but one in which we may freely swim; not a death-march on which we are prodded at gunpoint, but a path upon which we may freely walk? What if destiny is not a prison in which we have been born, but the gracious gift of a life and a future in which we have been set free to live?

I have already said that all lives have a shape; a curve; a trajectory. Another word for this is a *story*, and that is simply what I mean by destiny. We all find ourselves in a larger story which we ourselves did not write, yet in which we have real choices that make a difference in our lives and in the world around us. To put the same idea differently, all stories have already been written, but we still have to choose which story will be our own. All rivers run, through their curves, swamps, and rapids, inevitably to their oceans. Our question is, in which river are we sailing our boat? Or, if in fact our river is headed toward a deadly falls, will we abandon ship, grasp the rope thrown to us from the shore, and follow the one who leads to still waters? To be sure, all shapes have already been invented, and we certainly cannot create a new one for ourselves. But we are not yet done being shaped, and God is a merciful sculptor.

So it is that the Christian notion of destiny at once encompasses the past, the present, and the future. It is a future which has already been created by God's gracious actions in the past, and in which his people dwell in the present, even as they anticipate its full realization. To use the metaphor of shape, our destiny as believers is to one day be fully formed into a shape already created by God in the person of Jesus Christ, even as we grow to resemble him a little more each day. Christians are those who, by God's grace, have stepped out of their former destiny of separation from God, and into the new life which God has created in Christ. Such a destiny, far from being oppressive, is liberation itself. To consider the idea of destiny under such terms is to come closer to how Paul has described the Christian life in Philippians—a life shaped after the likeness of Christ.

Such a perspective, besides being biblical, is essential to a right self-understanding. As human beings, one of our most important tasks is to make sense of our own life; to answer questions like "Who am I? Where did I come from? Where am I going?" It is perhaps the case that all our assumptions, attitudes, habits, and behaviors can be traced back to how we answer these fundamental questions about ourselves. If we are interested in our own formation—that is, the kind of people we are becoming—we must attend to them. Spiritual formation in Christ is not at heart about the development of various practices, nor about weeding out besetting sins and vices. Although that is all necessarily involved, our Christian formation essentially comes down to knowing and embracing the reality in which we already live: the truths of God's loving creation, his gracious re-creation in Christ, and the future of redemption and glory which belongs to those who are united with him by faith. Before we get around to the important matters of what we do or don't do, we need to face the even more important matter of who and what we are. And here is one of the great and joyous secrets of the Christian life: that by the power of the Holy Spirit, we are in the process of becoming that which we already are. That which we were created to be, and which we already are in God's eyes through Christ, is now our true identity, and the day is coming—far or near—when we will really live like it.

Perhaps all of this seems rather theologically abstract. But it really comes down to this. As believers in Christ, we want to grow in becoming more like him. Or, at least we *want* to want that. We want to grow in grace and wisdom and righteousness and compassion. We want to cut out sinful habits that are destructive to ourselves and our relationships. We want to learn more self-control; in general, to grow toward that which has sometimes been called "victorious Christian living." From our everyday perspective, it seems like an insurmountable task, and even if we achieve progress in our moral development, we still run the deadly risk of becoming a self-righteous legalist.

But the great encouragement and empowerment for our Christian life is this: that we know we can change because we have already been changed. If we have beheld Christ, we have beheld our own source and our own final destiny. As Christians, our daily walk may take us through mists and swamps, but we know the road we are on is the one which leads to our goal—to God's goal. That is where we fix our eyes: not on the uncertainties of the moment but on the sureties of the gospel; that which God has already done through the cross to redeem us, and the guarantee of future redemption which this entails. This does not, however, mean ignoring the present, but rather seeing it all through fresh eyes. It means living in the moment, but in light of a future which God has already given us in Christ.

So it is that we begin our journey by looking to its end. Sometimes, counterintuitive as it may be, we need to begin at the end. When dealing with processes that are random or accidental, we cannot understand their end without first seeing their beginning and then each successive step of the process. But when dealing with processes that are intentional and goal-oriented, we cannot understand the beginning without having the end in view.

For example, think about the act of making a woodcarving (once again we think about the importance of shape and the process of being shaped). The woodcarver must take the first steps of his process, and each one successively, with a specific end already in view. The end product determines each step he takes, including those at the very beginning of his project.

So too with us. We cannot understand who we are—and indeed, what this whole world is—apart from God's final purpose for which he made us and all things. This purpose (for us, at least) is to be conformed to the image of God by being shaped after the likeness of his son Jesus Christ.

SHARING IN PAUL'S JOY

Perhaps now we can see more clearly what compels Paul to rejoice over this Philippian congregation, and in fact over everyone who shares their faith, even you and me. As is his habit, Paul begins by addressing them as God's "holy ones" (many translations use the more traditional term, "saints"). The more honest we are with ourselves, the less likely we are to regard ourselves as "holy." And yet, by being God's people in Christ, that is what we are. God has given us the identity of his holy, set-apart, Christ-shaped people. We may not always live this way perfectly, but God has drawn us into Christ and has therefore promised to transform us into his likeness. That is a matter for eternity—but no less for today.[1]

That is why Paul rejoices, all at once, in what the Philippians already are and in what they are destined in Christ to become. He is grateful for their participation in the gospel which they have shared from the very beginning of their relationship, and also— consequently, in fact—for the future completion of the good work which God has begun in them.

It's as simple as this: what God starts, he finishes. He is faithful and trustworthy. If he's started with us, then the day of our completion, remote as it may seem, is an unshakable promise of the omnipotent God! This is a constant and inextinguishable source of Christian hope.

This promise of God, the reality of which is already evident in the life of the Philippian church, elicits deep feelings of pastoral affection on Paul's part. He has personally experienced the reality of their faith in the form of their love and support for him, and he likewise longs to enjoy face-to-face communion with them.

God's promise of completion also informs Paul's prayer. He prays that their love, which he has already witnessed and experienced, will abound more and more, being ultimately directed toward their being "found blameless and true on the day of Christ." In other words, Paul prays that the Philippians will continue to become that which they already are; or, we could say, that they will continue to grasp in daily living that which is their final destiny (and therefore their present identity) through Christ.

But one of the most interesting things about this prayer for abounding love is that which their love is supposed to abound *in*:

1. "We have been transformed into the image of Christ, and are therefore destined to become like him. He is the only "pattern" we must follow." Bonhoeffer, *Cost of Discipleship*, 304.

knowledge and wisdom for discerning that which is worthy of their love. Paul doesn't merely pray that they will become more loving people (although surely that must be a part of it). He prays that their love will abound in the right direction—the direction of God's own heart. Here we encounter another crucial aspect of our formation toward Christlikeness: we must grow in learning to love the right things; namely, the things that God loves. We must grow in the discipline of rightly ordered desire.

THE ANATOMY OF DESIRE

It is one thing to be on a journey with a promised destination; it is another thing really to desire and long for that destination. It is one thing to have been promised Christlikeness; it is another to yearn for it in our life today. If we are in Christ, we know that God will be utterly faithful in realizing in our character the Christ-defined identity he has already given to us. God's desire for our life is clear as far as that is concerned. But what about our own desire? Do we want to receive God's gift of sanctification as much as God wants to give it?

Paul rejoiced in the way the Philippians participated together with him in the work of the gospel: the work of believing it, obeying it, enacting it, and preaching it. Here Paul's desire is in step with God's desire for all of us. God desires all of us to become active participants in the unfolding reality of what his gospel accomplishes in our lives. To do that, our hearts need to become aligned to his—delighting in his delights, loving what he loves, desiring what he desires, even hating what he hates.

But above all, our desire must be for Christ himself. For Christ did not come merely to teach us profound lessons of knowledge and goodness—although he did teach those things most excellently. He came to give us himself, to give himself up in death for us, and to rise from the grave in new life to share with all who believe. Insofar as we become sharers in his life—and indeed in his death—we become pulled toward him, around him in orbit, and into his very heart. We are now, though also not yet, *in Christ*, and that is the tension of the Christian life which must come to animate both our delight and our desire.

But what do we, in fact, desire? Is our love attuned to be able to discern that which is truly valuable, such that we love what God loves? To examine the desires of our own hearts is to engage in the dangerous, alarming, but ultimately life-giving endeavor of exposing our personal idolatries.

So again, what do we desire? We desire the love, respect, and admiration of our fellow human beings, especially those whose opinions particularly matter to us. We desire status, recognition, and accolades. We desire a well-earned break. We desire comfort and convenience—and the wealth that makes them possible. We desire knowledge and insight. We desire the actualization of our dreams. We desire to see our will done in the political realm, including the victory of our political heroes and the downfall of our political villains. And let's not forget the simple things: we desire food, sleep, a cool drink of water.

Of course, our list could reasonably progress much further—practically forever, in fact. But as we look at the short list we have created above, we already begin to observe that some objects of desire appear to be more appropriate than others. Some of these desires are good, others are less noble. Then of course we are reminded of our overtly sinful, wicked desires—for example, that secret, almost delicious longing for the humiliation of a person who has injured us.

But as we probe the anatomy of desire and seek to sort out that which is truly valuable, we must make a surprising observation: that there are no evil desires. There are only evil strategies for fulfilling them. Evil cannot create hunger, nor can it create the delicious morsel we crave. Hunger is part of the creator's design, and "every good and perfect gift comes from above." Evil can only place the morsel strategically as bait and wait for our desire to lead us into the trap. And unfortunately, we are all too willingly led. Evil, to say it again, is not so much a matter of wrong desires or desires for wrong things, but desiring the right things in the wrong ways and for the wrong reasons.

This is the logic of idolatry: we pursue the good things that come from God apart from God himself. We love the creation apart from rather than within the love of our creator. So it is that even the best things in life can become the objects of idolatrous lusts which tear our heart from the God who loves us; but so it also is that even the worst things in life, turned back to God, are refined in the creator's fire back into their God-glorifying form.

Take, for example, the worst desire we have listed above: the desire for revenge against someone who has done us wrong. We need to take Scripture's condemnation of vengeance absolutely seriously. But we also need to recognize that even within this wicked habit of the heart there is a seed of a godly desire: the longing for justice. Vengeance is, in fact, a satanic parody of justice. This means that a desire for justice is all too easily corrupted into bitter malice, but on the other hand, even bitter malice, by the grace of God, can be redeemed into a passion for the restoration of righteousness and the redemption of the wrongdoer.[2]

Or take another example: greed. We are quick to recognize the ugliness of the condition. But when a person is greedy, are they not desiring things that are, at least in their elemental forms, good? Money can be used perversely, and all too often is. But money itself is not evil. It is a representative share of the riches God has built into his earth, which he has meant for us to draw out, manage, and multiply for the flourishing of all creatures. Greed is poisonous because it seeks the goodness of wealth as a self-centered end rather than a God-centered means. In other words, greed seeks the happiness which inheres in the receiving and sharing of God's good things in those things themselves, and not in the love which animates them as gifts to be circulated in our human communion (we will return to this idea in chapter 8). We crave good things, and there is nothing wrong with the craving, unless it irrationally persists toward a perversity of excess, in which we have far more than we need while others go without. The person who selfishly hordes for himself, in a misguided desire for happiness, in fact deprives himself of the only way in which physical things can be involved

2. Allender and Longman, *Bold Love*, 183–204.

in human happiness: when they are shared as tokens of love and fellowship with God and others. So it is that idolatry spoils the very things we idolize. We heap on them the glory which only God is strong enough to bear, and they are crushed under the weight of our misguided praise. All good things we desire come from God; in God alone are all good desires fulfilled.

But how does one sort all these things out? Attuning our desires to godliness and pulling them out of our sinful, self-centered fulfillment strategies might seem like walking a tightrope, or perhaps wandering through a misty swamp. Perhaps it is. But any swamp is navigable if we have a compass that points true north. And that is what we have in Jesus Christ. He is the model in whose likeness we are being formed. All God's goodness is made visible in him, and he is the paradigm of God's purpose and destiny for humanity. Therefore he is the test of every desire. The question then is: are our desires compatible with what we see in Jesus Christ? Will there be any conflict between our desires (or our strategies for fulfilling them) and that which God will unveil on the day of Jesus Christ—the day of completion when God's people will be found blameless and true?

As we follow this passage in Philippians, we also see how worship is the test of our desires. Do our desires, in their present form, have their culmination and fulfillment in the glory and praise of God? This is how we can know if our hearts are properly attuned to that which has lasting and true value: if there is no conflict between what we desire and the pure worship of the true God in Jesus Christ. Here we are called to give all our desires back to the God who gave them in the first place, not that our desires may be put to death, but that they may be brought to true life in the only place of their fulfillment. This is near to the heart of God's message to us in his word: "Seek first the kingdom of God and his righteousness, and all these will be given to you" (Matt 6:33). "Delight yourself in the LORD, and he will give you the desires of your heart" (Ps 37:4).

So how can we partner with God in our journey of transformation toward our Christ-shaped destiny? We attune our hearts to the purposes of God which Christ has revealed. We seek first the future kingdom which has already set foot on earth in Jesus, and by doing so seek all good and worthwhile things. We delight in the worship of the most-high God, and thereby receive the desires of our heart. We lay all our desires down before his feet: not because they are bad and must be killed, but because they are good and must be resurrected. They must be redeemed out of their self-centered death, and into their God-given, God-glorifying form. We must learn to see all our wayward and foolish desires as the heart's muffled cry for its maker, and so seeing, turn again and again to him.

Above all, the God-glorifying form of our desires is manifested in love. Surely this must mean love for God, who has so extravagantly loved us in Jesus Christ. But this passage must also direct us toward rightly loving one another. Here Paul's prayer is striking: "May your love abound more and more in knowledge and depth of insight." We often regard love primarily as an affection of the heart or a feeling. But authentic love is so much more. It is a choice and an activity, and often a self-sacrificial one, for the good of others. Not only that: as this verse highlights, love includes a right attunement of the mind. Love, in other words, must be smart.

This calls for further reflection in our lives. We want to love others, but do we express love intelligently, insightfully, and with discernment? To add wisdom to love is not to diminish it. It does not mean holding something back in our love or scrutinizing whether a person is worthy. Our love must be like that of the God who gave his son; indeed who gave his very self: it must be both extravagant and clever. Perhaps all of this can be said more simply in the assertion that our love must hold nothing back from the resources God has given us: the resources of our mind, heart, and body. Indeed, this is how we are called to love God: with all our heart, soul, mind, and strength. Only so can we love our neighbor as we love ourselves. This is the only way we can learn to agree with God in desiring the destiny of completion after the pattern of Christ which he has given us.

CONCLUSION

A man once set off on a hike to the top of a mountain. In the morning, he looked up at the peak gleaming in the distance, and he began walking on the road which he knew came to its terminus at the summit. His journey was not, however, a straight and steady ascent. It led him through twists and turns around rocks, across perilous rapids, and through dark, misty valleys. But through his knowledge that he was on the right road, and the glimpses he caught along the way of the mountain peak standing tall and bright above him, even the darkest and most difficult moments of his journey were transformed from fearful wandering to a march of unfolding victory. That gave him the courage he needed to keep putting one foot in front of the other when things got tough. He began his journey, and persevered upon it, by looking to its end—his destiny of ascent.[3]

If we are in Christ, we are on such a journey. God is shaping our life, and while we are still bumpy and broken, our final shape has already been determined. We are destined to be shaped like Jesus Christ. God has called us to partner with him in the daily and eternal task of our transformation after the likeness of his son. We become more like Christ when we set our minds and hearts on the future destiny which God has already guaranteed in our present redemption. We become like Christ when we align our loves and desires with those of God.

God has a Christ-shaped destiny for our life. The question is, do we agree with God about where we are going? Are the desires of our hearts attuned toward the fulfillment of our salvation; and in fact, the fulfillment of all good things the heart desires? Do our hearts abound in love for that which has true value in the sight of God? And are we willing to cooperate with him in the daily task of being shaped into the likeness of his son, for whom all things were created, and in whom all good things are realized?

3. The imagery of this parable takes much inspiration from a piece of music: *Eine Alpensinfonie*, by Richard Strauss, which uses the language of symphonic composition to tell the story of a journey to the top of a mountain and back, as a kind of parable of the human life.

Lord, take my heart, and make it like to yours. For I confess that I do not love what I ought to love, and I do not love you as you deserve. My desire, O Lord, is that I would declare my love for you, and that my declaration would no longer be a lie. For you have loved me, fickle and faulty, with an everlasting love. You have held my unbelieving heart in the grip of your undying faithfulness. Your love is better than life—may my lips glorify you, and may my life declare your praise. So bend me, Lord, into the image of your son. Make me like clay in your hand, and my heart as molten iron in your crucible. For all good things come from you, and all that you make is good. You have set my feet upon the path of life. I have not the strength to climb, but you hold me by the hand and draw me closer every day. How I long for your presence, O Lord! Until the day when my eyes are so strengthened to behold your face, make the desire for you still unmet sweeter than any other fulfilled. Amen.

3

To Live Is Christ

The Christ-Shaped Life as Hope in Suffering

PHILIPPIANS 1:12–30

*Brothers and Sisters, I want you to know how the good news
has spread to the whole palace guard because of my chains—
my imprisonment is for the sake of Christ! My comrades in
the Lord here are also growing bolder to proclaim the gospel
because of my chains. Yes, some of them are doing so because
of envy and conflict with me, while others proclaim Christ for
true motives. The latter preach out of love, knowing that I have
been appointed to defend the gospel and desiring to share in
that task. The former preach Christ out of selfish ambition, not
sincerely, supposing they might exploit my imprisonment. But
what do they really accomplish? Surely just the furtherance of
the gospel, which progresses through false motives as well as
true! Either way, Christ is proclaimed, and I rejoice.*

*I also rejoice in the knowledge that this will turn out for
my deliverance—by means of your prayer and the spirit of*

Christ Jesus. This is my eager expectation and hope: that I will not be put to shame, but that I will be bold and confident, and that I will now and always exalt Christ in my body, whether by life or death. For me, to live is Christ and to die is gain. If my body lives, this means more fruitful work. So I hardly know which I would prefer and am hard-pressed to decide between the two. For I desire to depart and be with Christ, which is the greater thing by far, but my bodily life is of greater benefit for you. So I am confident that I will remain with you for the continuance of your joy and faith, so that I will live to stand again among you. Won't that be something worth boasting about in Christ!

Whatever in fact happens, may you continue to live your life in a manner worthy of the gospel of Christ, so that whether I come and see you myself, or else I hear a report about you from afar, I will know that you stand firmly together in one spirit, and with one mind continue in your struggle of faith for the gospel. Do not be intimidated by anything, including your opponents. God has given a sign that they will be destroyed, but that you will be saved: he has granted to you not only to believe in Christ, but to suffer on his behalf. Indeed, you are going through the same struggle you have seen me face, and which I continue to face.

THE DISCIPLINE OF HOPE

IN THE PREVIOUS CHAPTER, we pondered the notion of destiny from a distinctly Christian perspective, as informed by God's promise to complete the work in us which he has already begun. Here we gain the strength to take up our cross each day by looking to the final destination which God has already guaranteed in Christ. Having such a God-given destiny is not a matter of fate or determinism, but the gift of a Christ-shaped future which God has opened before us and made possible by his constant presence with us. It does not call for passivity on our part, but rather an eager partnership with God in which we attune our desires, by the renewing power of his Spirit, to their true object: "Christ in us, the hope of glory" (Col 1:27). All desires are ultimately given by God and fulfilled in him. We need to give them back to him so that they may be resurrected into their God-glorifying form and cleansed of their idolatrous, self-centered misdirections. This is the discipline of cultivating well-ordered desire; of allowing God to make our love abound in knowledge and depth of insight so that we are able to discern that which has eternal value, and so that the yearnings of our hearts are pulling in the direction of God's promised redemption. In short, we give our desires to God to be pulled toward the pattern of Christ, such that when heaven arrives, we are not in fact disappointed by what we then receive from God.[1]

There is a deeply biblical word which much more briefly and simply encapsulates all of this: *hope*. As Christians, who are called to embrace the Christ-shaped life which we have already been given and which is God's final promise, we are called to engage in the discipline of hope. To hope, in the biblical sense, does not mean merely to wish for a possibility, but to anticipate and live in light of God's promised reality.

But as we consider the discipline of hope, we encounter a paradox: the discipline of Christ-shaped hope means, in the here

---

1. A word of explanation is in order regarding the word *heaven* as it occurs here and elsewhere throughout this book. I do not mean to suggest, as has been believed by many Christians throughout history, that the eternal home of God's people is an immaterial afterlife. The teaching of Scripture is that God first intended, and still intends, for his people to inhabit this earth. The hope of the gospel is a physical resurrection into the renewed heavens and earth, where we will live forever in the community of God and fulfill our creation-calling to rule the earth as agents of God's blessing and glory. Here and elsewhere I use the word *heaven* in what I take to be its more biblical sense: the coming realm of God which is already a reality in Christ, but will one day be fully established on the earth. We are already citizens of heaven, yet we await the day on which heaven will descend to earth and we will become fully remade after the pattern of Christ. For a full treatment of this discussion, see Middleton, *New Heaven and a New Earth*.

and now, to embrace the discipline of Christ-shaped suffering. To be resurrected with him means also to be crucified with him. As the old saying goes, "no cross, no crown."[2]

But the good news is this: that the Christian life, envisioned as such, is not a dreary death-march, but is in fact a joyous celebration of God's power and love, for it was on the cross that these were, mysteriously, most perfectly magnified. This is the paradox of the gospel: "For whoever wants to save their life will lose it, but whoever loses their life for me will find it" (Matt 16:25). This is in fact the paradox of love. To love sincerely is to involve ourselves in the suffering of others, but such love, in which one forsakes their own happiness, is the only path to true joy.

PAUL'S SUFFERINGS, PAUL'S JOY

These ideas are deeply embedded in Philippians 1:12–30, in which we are confronted with what at first seems like an exceedingly odd juxtaposition: suffering and joy. It's common knowledge, for those well acquainted with the New Testament, that the epistle to the Philippians is an ebulliently joyful letter. But it seems strange to us to see so much joy, celebration, and thanksgiving here attached to such painful and bitter circumstances.

Those circumstances seem to be shared by Paul and his audience. Paul himself writes from prison. Perhaps this was a situation of house arrest; evidently he had enough freedom to pen letters during his incarceration. And yet Paul's situation, by all indication in this passage, must have been extremely difficult. He indicates that there is some form of antagonism or rivalry against him on the part of some people, who for reasons and by methods unknown to us were using the gospel as a weapon against him. Yet he was able to rejoice in this, seeing God's hand at work even through people who were working for less than noble motives. Then there is the implication that Paul's life itself is in serious danger, as he contemplates the possibilities of living or dying. Although he seems to

2. This phrase comes from (or at least is best known as) the title of a work by the Quaker writer William Penn.

have a strong sense of confidence that he will survive the situation, he faces the possibility of death not with stoic resignation, but with an attitude that is downright cheery. Then toward the end of the passage, Paul indicates that those to whom he writes are also facing some form of suffering or persecution at the hands of opponents. And again, this is greeted not as a cause for consternation, but celebration. How can this be?

There are a few different answers to this question which appear throughout the passage. Paul regards his imprisonment not as a discouraging setback for his ministry and that of his comrades, but quite the opposite, noticing how it opens unique opportunities to preach the gospel to an unlikely audience (the palace guard), and also provides an emboldening influence on those around him.

Paul is also thankful for the work of gospel-preaching opponents rather than offended, angered, or distressed, because his priority really is the furtherance of the gospel. We have already reflected on the subtle dynamics of human desires and the need to discern whether they are being directed toward their God-designed and Christ-redeemed object, and there is no better example than what we find here. Had Paul's desires been fixated on his own pride and the advancement of his personal career, he would not have been able to take any pleasure in rival ministries. Paul's delight in the progress of the gospel, however it is coming about, is proof that his love has abounded in knowledge and depth of insight, so as to approve that which has true value.

Then there is Paul's cheery attitude toward death. Paul is not the only ancient figure to be sanguine toward the prospect of his own demise. We think of certain Greek philosophical schools of thought, such as stoicism, which praised the ability to maintain an unaffected composure in all events, whether good or ill. We also think about the story related by Plato in *The Last Days of Socrates*, in which the philosopher explains to his friends why he does not fear death but rather welcomes it as an escape from bodily imprisonment and an entrance into a more perfect and enlightened state of being.[3] But neither of those are Paul's reasons. His positive

3. Plato, *Phaedo*, 111–12.

attitude toward the possibility of death is solely because of his savior, Jesus Christ. Death is not good in itself, nor to be desired as a means of escape from an evil world, nor yearned for as a path to enlightenment, nor treated as an occasion for stoic pride, but is greeted positively only in light of the promised presence of Jesus Christ. Paul knows that "to be absent from the body is to be present with the Lord." Death therefore holds no terror for him, not because of philosophical rejections of bodily life, but because of the powerful promise of the resurrected Christ.

Finally, Paul shares his highly encouraging point of view with his Philippian audience regarding their own trials and persecutions. He seems to recast their suffering as a gift of divine honor, saying that "God has given a sign that they will be destroyed, but that you will be saved: he has granted to you not only to believe in Christ, but to suffer on his behalf."

We shouldn't too quickly brush past the apparent strangeness of Paul's juxtaposition of suffering and joy. Perhaps many Christians are too hasty in trying to cast their sufferings in a positive light without really coming to terms emotionally with what they are experiencing. We can all too quickly resort to easy quips about how "this must just be part of God's plan" or "I better not be anxious, but just trust God." Of course, these can be statements of deep faith, but sometimes they are, in reality, a spiritual-sounding excuse to avoid the challenge of dealing honestly with what we are facing. God surely desires our faith and our trust, but he also desires our honesty. In fact, authentic faith and trust are not marked by the absence of fear or anxiety, but rather a willingness to acknowledge them in the presence of God, and in so doing, remain faithful to him even when it is most difficult. That is the real meaning of courageous faith.

So, in reading about Paul's imprisonment, his ministry challenges, the impending possibility of his death, and the persecutions of his Philippian audience, we shouldn't jump to the quick-and-easy conclusion that such difficulties can be interpreted simplistically as blessings. In fact, they can be interpreted as blessings, but neither easily nor naturally. Suffering is real, it is ugly, and—to put it bluntly—it is evil. Suffering is part of the condition of a fallen world awaiting restoration. Paul's joyful perspective here is not the expression of an optimistic disposition, a naively buoyant faith, or a failure to reckon with the reality of evil. The juxtaposition between suffering and joyful hope which we see here is so strong a paradox that it can only be sustained by the power of an even greater paradox: the victorious suffering of Christ upon the cross. The joy amid suffering which Paul describes here can only legitimately exist as an expression of the gospel.

And that is, in fact, the logic which underlies this passage. Imprisonment, opposition by troublemakers, persecution, and death are each, in their own way, glorified by their connection with the gospel of Jesus Christ. Paul's imprisonment advanced the gospel. The misguided preaching of his rivals advanced the gospel. The suffering of his Philippian brothers and sisters was a partnership in suffering on behalf of the gospel. For Paul, even death itself was an expression of the cruciform gospel of Jesus Christ. It is by this, and this alone, that such sufferings are transfigured into joy. For Paul, for the Philippians, and for us, suffering becomes hope only when it is enfolded into the Christ-shaped life.

For Paul—and for us too, if we are willing—suffering in obedience to Christ is a discipline of hope. Paul describes this more clearly in Romans 8:18–25, in which he argues that "our present sufferings are not worth comparing with the glory that will be revealed in us." He describes how not only we, but the entire creation, is yearning for "the children of God to be revealed." In the meantime, we learn the discipline of waiting patiently, hoping for that which we do not yet have. Suffering in this way calls our minds and our hearts toward the blessed future in which God has included us. It teaches us to pray with the Lord Jesus Christ: "Thy kingdom come, thy will be done on earth, as it is in heaven." It teaches us to share the heart of God by grieving for a broken world, by yearning for the day of its full redemption, and by participating, already but not yet, in the death and resurrection of the one who has already won the victory.

SUFFERING AND SANCTIFICATION

There are many more specific ways in which suffering, though in itself an evil, can play a role in our formation toward Christlikeness. We all know that suffering has the potential to build moral, emotional, and relational strength. This is not a given. But for those who see suffering as an opportunity to identify with the crucified Christ, it will teach them to see themselves and the world more through his eyes. The experience of suffering reminds us of the fallen state of the world, and our own brokenness, and therefore points us toward our need for a savior. In this way, it can function like the thirst which drives us to drink from the well of God's promises, or like the pain in our body which tells us to seek out a doctor. (Of course, there are perils along the way. Sin consists of trying to quench the thirst of our brokenness with the saltwater which the world offers in abundance, or in trying to patch ourselves up with quick fixes rather than attending to our underlying condition which can only be mended by our maker.) In alerting us to the realities of evil, sin, and oppression in the world, suffering also serves as a summons to courageous, loving action in the name of the healer, Jesus Christ. After all, suffering must not merely make us hunger to escape the world's pain by fleeing toward a distant heaven, but move us to embrace the redemptive lifestyle of heaven which God means for us to model here and now.

Finally, to suffer as a Christian is to be a witness to the truth of the gospel. To face difficulties, pains, and trials in this world while grasping the hand of Christ is to share the heart of the redeeming God. If we face suffering with faith and courage, we are testifying to the truth that that Jesus Christ is the crucified conqueror. We bear witness to that unshakable foundation which is the kingdom of God, rather than the shifting sands of worldly comfort.

Perhaps in light of all this we can better understand Jesus's counterintuitive introduction to the Sermon on the Mount:

Blessed are the poor in spirit, for theirs is the kingdom
of heaven.
Blessed are those who mourn, for they will be comforted.

Blessed are the meek, for they will inherit the earth.
Blessed are those who hunger and thirst for righteousness,
for they will be filled.
Blessed are the merciful, for they will receive mercy.
Blessed are the pure in heart, for they will see God.
Blessed are the peacemakers, for they will be called
children of God.
Blessed are those who are persecuted because of righteousness,
for theirs is the kingdom of heaven (Matt 5:3–10).

To suffer, if we suffer as members of God's kingdom, is evidence that we are part of the right company; that we have invested in stock of lasting value. It's evidence that we haven't built our life on the foundation of physical comfort and worldly pleasure, which is fleeting at best, but rather on that of the eternal comfort and pleasure of God, which has been established for us in the life, death, and resurrection of Jesus Christ.

To paraphrase the one who suffered and died for us that we might live, *those who try to preserve their lives (or their comfort) will lose it, but those who lay down their lives (and their comfort) for the sake of Christ and his kingdom will find lasting life and true comfort.* We sabotage our spiritual formation, and indeed our own true happiness, when we make the avoidance of suffering our chief aim in life. Paul takes suffering in his life as evidence of the triumph of the gospel and an honor bestowed by God. For Paul, suffering is the discipline of hope; of joyfully anticipating God's victorious kingdom, even as he partners with Christ in enacting this kingdom in the present world by the power of the Holy Spirit.

CONCLUSION: TO LIVE IS CHRIST

For the Christian, to live is Christ, and therefore to die is gain. Jesus Christ is the source and the goal of our life, and the shape of everything in between. To live Christianly, then, means to suffer after the pattern of the one who achieved victory by dying on the cross. But such suffering means, from the point of view of God's kingdom, to be truly alive; really to be a participant in

God's redemptive work in the world. Therefore suffering, for the Christian, is the discipline of anticipating the resurrection—the discipline of hope.

Of course, not every Christian life is the same. Many of us are privileged not to face persecution, or to have a relatively safe and comfortable life. That is something for which to give thanks. It would be a distortion of this teaching to embrace a kind of Christian masochism in which we deliberately seek out pain, suffering, and persecution so as to affirm our Christian identity.[4] That identity has been established for us already in what Christ suffered, and nothing needs to be added for the completion of that great task. We think about the tendency among some in the ancient and medieval church to make martyrdom an end in itself and to glorify poverty and suffering in ways that seem perverse to us.

We rightly reject this line of thought, but perhaps we, in our modern context, are just as far from the truth in the opposite direction. We instinctively believe that the point of life is to be as comfortable as possible, mistakenly thinking that true happiness is defined by the avoidance of pain. A successful life, according to modern people of religious as well as secular stripes, is one in which we experience financial plenty, good health, and in general smooth sailing from womb to tomb. Again, such a life is no bad thing and those who experience it should be grateful, but it is hardly to be seen as the defining mark of those people who are identified with Jesus Christ. True happiness, from a Christian point of view, means knowing the joy of union with God through the crucified and risen Christ, and living a life whose entire shape is derived from his redeeming ministry.

So again, the point is not to seek out pain and persecution (nor to glory in the false perception of them), but rather to seek out Christ—whatever the cost. Such a life is not marked by grim resignation, but joyful hope, for the basis of our life is the unbreakable promise of God. Our hope, our joy, our desire, is the promise

---

4. We should also beware of the tendency to think of ourselves as persecuted when we are merely faced with disagreements, inconveniences, or the absence of privilege.

of a Christ-defined life, rather than the fleeting prospects of physical comfort.

This means that such pains as we may face in life—and everyone encounters pain and suffering throughout life, in some degree or another—can be recognized as opportunities for spiritual formation after the likeness of Christ. Here suffering, pain, and grief are still regarded as evils and evidences of a broken creation, yet redeemable by God as tools for pulling us toward our God-given destiny. God has not destined us to suffer, and pain is not a part of his original plan. But in and through Christ, God has made pain and suffering work on behalf of his plan. Like a wise warrior, he uses his enemy's own strength against him.

That is the battle in which we now fight. The question, as we have already said, is whether our desires and our delights are growing to match God's own. It is not a matter of learning to delight in suffering or to desire pain, but rather of learning to see all things in life, including such pain and suffering as comes our way, as opportunities to desire God and to delight in his son. To live with such an attitude is to live in a manner worthy of the one whose name we bear.

> Lord,
> May we then know the more of love,
> The more of death and earthly pain,
> For he who died now reigns above,
> With both scars and crown to prove:
> "To live is Christ, to die is gain!"
> Amen.

4

May Your Mind Be That of Christ Jesus

The Christ-Shaped Life as Humble Servant Love

PHILIPPIANS 2:1–11

Therefore, if you have any comfort in Christ, any consolation in his love, any fellowship in the Spirit, any affection and compassion, make my joy complete by being likeminded, sharing the same love and being united in one spirit and one mind. Do not live in selfish ambition or vain conceit, but in humility put one another above your own selves. Don't just look out for your own interests, but for the interests of each other. Have the same mind among you as that of Christ Jesus:

Who though God in very being, did not regard himself as God's equal,

But emptied himself in the manner of a servant, becoming human flesh.

He humbled himself, becoming obedient to death, and even death on a cross.

Therefore God exalted him and bestowed upon him the name that is above every name,

So that at the name of Jesus every knee should bow, in heaven, on earth, and below the earth,

And every tongue confess that Jesus Christ is Lord, to the glory of God the Father.

THE HUMILITY OF GOD

THERE IS NO HUMILITY like the humility of God.

Humility gets a bad rap in today's world. We sing the liturgy that says "blessed are the assertive, for they shall get what they want. Blessed are the ones who demand their own rights, for they shall never stoop before others. Blessed are those who believe in themselves, for they shall inherit the earth."

Jesus sang a different tune: "Those who exalt themselves will be humbled, and those who humble themselves will be exalted." But he didn't just say it. He lived it, and he lived it like no other, through his incarnation, life, death, and resurrection.

If anyone has the right to be proud, it's Jesus. After all, he is the very fullness of God; the one in whom God has most fully and gloriously revealed himself. But it turns out that God's greatness and glory is expressed, surprisingly, in his humility. There is only one being in the universe who deserves to be self-centered, and he has chosen to be more other-centered than any of his creatures can imagine. After all, the lower one is, the more room for unwarranted pride, and the greater one is, the more room for unexpected humility. There is no pride like the pride of sinful human beings, and there is no humility like the humility of God.

That's part of the mystery of God: never was he more glorious, more Godlike, more *himself*, than when, in the body of Jesus Christ, he hung powerless and defeated on a Roman cross for the sake of love. This has profound significance for our own journey toward Christlikeness. We are never more like Jesus Christ—and therefore, never more like God—than when we live in self-sacrificial humility for others.

THE CHRIST-SHAPED TRAJECTORY: DOWN AND UP AGAIN

Throughout the second half of Philippians 1, Paul has celebrated how even suffering is an occasion for joy when it is part of a gospel-centered, Christ-shaped life. Here in chapter 2, he describes the deeper substance of this claim, which is the profound mystery of Jesus's incarnation, servitude, death, resurrection, and glorification. Paul has already described how he has, in some small measure, modeled this Christ-shaped life through his own sufferings for the sake of the gospel. He's also enjoined his Philippian audience to view their own sufferings in the same light, calling them to live a life worthy of the savior whose name they bear. But this reality is not only visible in overt sufferings and persecutions. It is meant to be put on display throughout the whole Christian life, in everyday relationships of self-giving love and humble service. Paul invokes no less staggering a picture than the death and resurrection of Christ to exemplify such a seemingly simple aspect of daily living.

Perhaps humility is well-acknowledged as a Christian virtue. But we don't always think deeply about what humility really means. This passage gives us a clarifying definition. Humility does not mean belittling ourselves or sticking our faces in the dirt. It doesn't mean downplaying any virtue or talent we might possess. Most strictly speaking, humility is not even best defined as the absence of pride. Rather it is the presence of self-sacrificial love. Humility does not mean lowering oneself as an end-in-itself, but doing what is necessary to bring honor and flourishing to others— even at one's own expense if necessary. It means regarding other people and what is best for them as more important than our own personal desires or interests.

Humility therefore means a kind of other-centeredness. This puts it at odds not only with pride, but also with the kind of false humility which is actually just an alternative way of being self-centered. Such false humility may lead us to make apparently loving sacrifices for other people, all with a kind of morose grandiosity. But true humility finds its sincerest delight simply in the good of others.

A person whose heart is filled with this kind of humility delights in self-sacrifice for the wellbeing of someone else, such that it hardly feels like a self-sacrifice at all. This goes against certain modern intuitions about unselfishness; namely that the ideal unselfish act is one done for the good of others but which gives no benefit or pleasure to oneself. I think this is very far from the truth. True unselfishness—or better, true love—is the act of doing good for another, even at one's own expense, and finding it all a sublime joy. The truly humble, loving, and unselfish person is the kind of person whose greatest joy is the wellbeing of others. For such a person, there is no difference between self-denying kindness and the pursuit of happiness. To be such a person is to be, in ever so small a measure, like the God who most fully affirmed himself when he emptied himself for love's sake.

Of course, we have a long way to go. Some of us may boast that we have attained such towering heights of humility. Others of us know the truth. But if all that has been said thus far holds true, and we who bear Christ's name are already destined to be like him, such self-emptying love is indeed the shape of our future life. By God's grace, it may even begin to inhabit our present.

Indeed, here in Philippians chapter 2 is where we most directly behold the meaning of the Christ-shaped life. Lest all this talk about *shape* be thought a mere metaphor, this passage quite literally describes a trajectory which could be drawn in an instant with paper and ink: simply think of an inverted arch; a down-and-up-again swoosh.

Down and up again: that was God's mighty path, which he journeyed in the flesh and blood of Jesus Christ, and that too is the road of all who follow in his train. God has come down for us; down from highest heaven to his wayward world, and into the fray of death itself. But this journey was not for him alone: like a rescue diver, he has plunged himself into the depths, and drawn us up with him. Therefore the Christian life, in its whole form, is a humbleness destined unto glory. It is the great theme of our play which is woven into every simplest scene of life. To give oneself, to break one's heart for a world in need, to give a cup of water, to stop a moment for a stranger, to love, is to grasp the nail-pierced hand of the living God and find oneself pulled into the orbit of his glory. There is no discipline of the Christian life so simple yet so Godlike as the discipline of humility.

Of course, we mustn't let humility go to our heads, or we shatter the whole thing. We are best off, I believe, not by pursuing humility itself, but letting it grow wild in the garden which is watered by love. Let us learn to love, and we will find ourselves a truer window by which to see the world, and indeed a better mirror by which to see ourselves in it.

For pride is, in fact, basically a distorted view of reality. Pride is a guilty forgetfulness of the great facts about reality; about who God is and who we are. This is why the Scriptures consistently depict wisdom as beginning with "the fear of the Lord," which is essentially a humility before the God-ness of God; a recognition of who and what he is and therefore who and what we are by contrast. Wisdom, and humility, basically consist in living one's whole life on the basis of these facts. The age-old problem of pride takes many devious forms, but it always involves forgetting the truths of who God is and who we are.

We may forget these things in more than one way. We may succumb to the hubris of becoming gods to ourselves, according to the temptation of the serpent and the aspirations of the tower-builders at Babel. Or we may lie to ourselves in a different way by thinking ourselves worthless and despised, and by wallowing in self-pity. But this too is a prideful distortion of reality; a centering of our world around something other than the true center. Pride means being a self-centered being in a God-centered universe. Any form of self-centeredness, whether the self is celebrated or despised, is a distorted picture of reality. It is a planet imagining itself to be a star—or perhaps a black hole—rather than joyfully embracing its reality as a reflector of the light of its sun.

So the way to humility must not be a preoccupation with lowering ourselves, and therefore merely adapting a new way of being self-centered, but rather a jubilant admiration of God and a joyful obedience to the creatureliness he has bestowed upon us. That gives us the right picture of reality. But again, the best way to see this picture clearly is through the lens of love. That is why the heart of the whole law is "Love the Lord your God with all your heart, soul, mind, and strength, and love your neighbor as yourself." We do not rightly comprehend the height of God's glory unless we are gazing at the depths of his love. This love was made visible in the lowliest and darkest of places: the cross. Adam and Eve accepted a distorted picture of reality when they believed the lie of the serpent, in which God could not be trusted to act for their good. In contrast, we receive the clearest picture of reality when we see the love of God poured out for us upon the cross. It is only then that we can begin to live according to the great facts of reality. When we do that, and our lives are going with the grain of the God-centered universe rather than against it, we will love the God who loves us, and we will love our neighbors, whom he loves.

IT'S NOT ABOUT ME

How do we practice this in everyday life? What does the song of God's self-emptying love sound like when played upon the simple instrument of our daily existence in the world? We have already praised the greatness of humility and explained how it is manifest in other-centered, Christ-defined love. But perhaps the commandment of Philippians 2 can best be said this way: "It's not about me."

It almost goes without saying that we tend to be self-centered creatures. Now in one sense, there's nothing wrong with this. It's even part of God's good design. God made us to have "selves." When God created the world, he made human beings stewards of it, responsible for its care and management. And there's a sense in which the first thing over which we are given such responsibility is our own selves. All of us are rightly self-centered in the sense that we each see the world from the vantage point of our own personal existence, as a captain sees the ocean from the prow of his ship. To have a self, and to live life from the center of that self, is no bad thing. It's just how God created us, and in fact, it's impossible not to live this way, barring some form of self-annihilation—an idea known to some eastern religions but foreign to the Christian Scriptures.

But here's the issue: how exactly, and for what purposes, have we gone about managing our selves? How have we captained our ships? Have we done so in service to God and love for one another? Are we operating as captains of vessels in God's great armada, or more like rogue pirates, plundering the seas on our own terms? We cannot see the world except through the eyes, brain, and soul which God has given us, but in what manner has this seeing been undertaken? Have we used our eyes as instruments of lust, or of grateful admiration? Have we used our brains as devices of deception and manipulation, or for creativity and intelligence in the service of God's glory and the flourishing of his world? Have we treated our souls as vessels of God's glory and love, or as things whose desires must be fulfilled on no terms but our own? In short, we can all ask ourselves, "How have I managed *me*?" It's no bad thing to live life as an *I* or a self. We really don't have any other option. But are our lives all *about* me—or about something bigger?

That's the important question: have I made the world around me all about myself, or have I made myself about God and the world of which he is king? How have I managed the *me* God has created?

Unfortunately, as we've already noted, it's instinctive for us to be self-centered creatures in a God-centered universe. We've lived for our own purposes rather than his. We've tried to get good, God-created things without God himself. We've attempted to satisfy God-given desires, of which he alone is the ultimate satisfaction, on self-sufficient, unbelieving terms. We've all "considered equality with God something to be grasped," making petty little gods of ourselves, even as the real God has offered himself to us in all his infinite bounty.

And it all plays out in our everyday instinct to make everything all about *me*. That's the sting of Paul's words: *"Do not live in selfish ambition or vain conceit, but in humility put one another above your own selves. Don't just look out for your own interests, but for the interests of each other."* We're called to view other people as more important than ourselves. But it doesn't take a great deal of self-examination to realize how poor we are at doing this. Surely most of us care about other people some of the time, perhaps even most of the time. But what happens in those moments when our guard is down; perhaps simply when we're tired, hungry, or stressed out? Those moments tend to reveal our default state, where once again, it's all about *me*.

Imagine, only too briefly, a few examples. My spouse asks me if I can help with a chore while I am preoccupied with something during what I regard as "my own time." I get a phone call from someone I know is lonely, I've got time to talk to them, but I'm tired and this person wears me down. Someone just ahead of me at the supermarket takes the last of that item on my list I was hoping to get. A pedestrian crosses the street in front of me and forces me to miss the green light. Whatever I end up doing in response, what are my instinctive internal reactions in moments like these?

But God is really sculpting us, chip by chip, into the image and likeness of his son, Jesus Christ. This means that a day is coming, sooner or later, when we will truly and instinctively live for the good of others, delighting even to lower ourselves for their honor. The down-and-up-again path will be the highway of our heart. Imagine what glorious fellowship and communion that will be, when everyone lives for all, and all live for the glory and praise of the God who gives his all for us!

Until that day, how do we live? Perhaps that is a question which can only be answered in volumes. But I will offer three short observations which are hopefully pertinent.

Work on Our Habits

First, Christians have always recognized that virtue, like a muscle, requires regular exercise to grow in strength. This is certainly true of servant love. We are not naturally or instinctively interested in the good of others before ourselves, but it is possible for this to change gradually by the influence of habit. Our final goal—and Christ's—is for us to become the kind of people who put others first as a matter of disposition and delight, with our outer behavior flowing naturally from an inward attitude. But it is not always possible to begin this way. Sometimes we need to start with the outward behaviors, which become the scaffolding supporting the rising structure of a renewed heart. If we make a practice of intentionally acting the part of self-giving, servant love for those around us, it will make its way into our character over time.

Do Great Things Humbly and Humble Things Greatly

This leads to a second (twofold) observation about our behavior in daily life: the Christian should be a person who does great things humbly and humble things greatly. What is an activity or skill at which we excel, and in which we are likely to pride ourselves? We ought to develop the ability to do these things with the excellence that gives us and others joy, but without the sounding of a trumpet. We need to learn to do our best things quietly, for their own sake, for that of others, and for the Lord to whom they are owed, and not for recognition and accolades.

At the same time, a humble person will do humble things greatly. He or she will not think it beneath himself or herself to invest thoughtful care or vigorous energy into even a very little thing that brings some good to others.

At the heart of all this is the observation that humility is not merely a passive thing. Humility is not merely the absence of pride, but the presence of love, and love is an activity of both body and soul. To love, or to be other-centered, involves not just affections of the heart, but also works of the hands. The larger picture of humility, in which we do humble things greatly and great things humbly, involves being passionately and excellently invested in realities larger than ourselves. Indeed there is, perhaps to our surprise, a kind of humility inherent in truly excellent work, for in doing something excellently for its own sake we are caught up in a world bigger than ourselves. Humility brings us to the end of ourselves, but therefore to the beginning of everything else.

This strikes at the heart of much self-centeredness in the modern age. The culture of our contemporary world has a deep bent toward self-centeredness, although not just in the sense of individual selfishness and the prioritization of self-fulfillment over servant love. These are real problems, but I believe that they are perhaps symptomatic of a deeper issue, in which we have been taught to spend much of our thought-life looking in a mirror. Rather than looking out upon the world around us through the lens of our God-given selves, we have learned to look in upon ourselves through the lenses supplied by the world. There are, of course, healthy and spiritually necessary forms of self-examination, in which we consider our own thoughts, affections, and desires. But this easily becomes exaggerated into an unhealthy preoccupation with ourselves. Sometimes this takes the form of conceited vanity or megalomania, but perhaps just as often it is manifest in poor self-image and insecurity, in which we constantly worry whether we are good enough compared to other people. In such a frame of mind, the excellence we see in another person is not a cause for joyful admiration, but rather anxiety about our ability to measure up to them. Of course, this can go the opposite direction too, in which we see the faults of others as occasions for a secret celebration of our own superiority. In any case, we make the people around us, and in fact the whole world around us, into a series of psychological events which are all about ourselves, whether in a positive or negative sense. All of life becomes an endless hall of mirrors in which to gaze at ourselves, in vanity and despair.

It is for this reason that there is a special need for God's people to learn the discipline of humility, in which we embrace the adventure of living into realities larger than ourselves. The evidence of such a life consists not only in acts of personal self-sacrifice, but the pattern of life in which we do humble things greatly, giving ourselves even to little tasks that are worth doing, while also doing great things humbly, in which we become self-forgetful participants in a great mission larger than ourselves. In this sense, there is tremendous spiritual value in attending earnestly to honest work, and even in the enjoyment of a good hobby.

Reflect Often on the Beauty of Christ

A third and perhaps most important observation about the daily discipline of humility is our need to reflect often on the beauty of Christ and what he has done for us. Once again, this draws our eyes away from the mirror and onto the true reality in which we live, which is God's drama of redemptive love. We cannot grow in humility by obsessing over how humble we are. That is the paradox of pride. But the inverse of this is the paradox of love, in which we are strongest when we spend our strength for others, most beautiful when we forget ourselves in admiration of something beautiful, and happiest when we forget our happiness in the pursuit of something bigger than ourselves. So it is that we are most filled with Christlike humility not when we are thinking about humility, but when we are thinking of Christ. The point is to live for something larger than ourselves: to think about things greater than our own thoughts; to act for things greater than our own actions; for our lives to be enfolded into a drama which is greater than our own story. That is the meaning of humility, and perhaps the true meaning of love: to become oneself in living for something beyond oneself. When we fix our eyes on Christ and follow in his footsteps, we are not only perceiving the ultimate example of humble love. We are also being taken beyond ourselves into the worthiest cause of all: the glory and honor of the most-high God. This is what we do when we turn our hearts to Christ and contemplate the riches of his redeeming love. When we ponder his incarnation, death, and resurrection, we are fixing our eyes on the glorious humility of

God. And not only that: we are also contemplating our own story which he has already written for us.

CONCLUSION: TO SING THAT MIGHTY CHORD

Man, for the sake of pride, said "I shall become God." God, for the sake of love, said "I shall become man." But the implications of this great truth are less symmetrical. In our great presumption to divine authority, we as humans have rejected our own good, God-given humanity. But in God's act of stooping to take on humanity, he did not reject his divinity. Rather, he affirmed it—paradoxically, yet gloriously.

This brings to mind an old theological dispute about the idea of *kenosis*, which centers around the ideas presented in Philippians 2. The word *kenosis* is derived from the Greek verb *kenao*, which means "to empty," and it appears in Philippians 2:7, which says that Christ "emptied himself." But what exactly did he "empty himself" of? In the context, it appears to be the honor due him as one who is "by very nature God" and the right to enjoy the benefits of equality with the Father. Instead, he took the position of a lowly servant. Some translations read "he made himself nothing." Some have argued that Christ actually emptied himself of divinity, such that he ceased, for a time, to be divine. Now perhaps a good case can be made that Jesus of Nazareth gave up the *use* of his divine attributes such as omniscience, omnipotence, and omnipresence, so as to depend completely on the Father and enter total solidarity with finite humanity. I think that a study of the Gospels suggests this to be the case. But that is a far cry from an emptying of divinity. The essence of divinity is not, after all, a set of impressive attributes. It is the Trinity, which is an eternal communion of perfect love. From beyond all time, God has been a fellowship of three persons bound together in loving union of being. We may imagine Father, Son, and Holy Spirit from all eternity pouring themselves into one another in self-giving love. (Some suggest that the word *kenao* has a connotation of the action of pouring out, like water from a pitcher, calling to mind the great statement in Isaiah 53:12

that "he poured out his life unto death.") If that is the truth about God, never did he so wondrously affirm his God-ness than when he emptied himself and laid down his right to be treated like God. Never did God so perfectly reveal and express himself as when he hung naked and powerless upon the cross to die for his enemies, all for the sake of love. In amazing irony, it was when Christ laid down his right to sing his part in the great song of trinitarian glory, that he in fact sang it out the loudest, for the trinitarian song is one of self-giving love.[1]

That divine reality of love is also the model for us to imitate. In fact, it is the paradigm of our new life of union with Christ. When we embrace that kind of self-giving, servant love which pursues the good of others even at high cost to ourselves, we are taking up, once again, our true humanity in which we bear the image of the trinitarian God.

And now the drama has come full circle: man, for the sake of pride, said "I shall become God." God, for the sake of love, said "I shall become man." Therefore man, by the love of God in Christ, has become man once more, man in the image and likeness of God, man swept into the very cloud of God's glory. Man has been prideful, God has been humble. Man has been humbled, and God has lifted him up. Now mankind rejoices, and God is forever praised.

That is the meaning of this great passage in Philippians 2. It has already been given a paraphrase above, but a song such as this deserves yet another:

> *May your mind be that of Christ the Lord,*
> *Who, though God before all space and time,*

---

1. Michael Gorman argues that the phrase in Phil 2:6, "*Although* he was in the form of God," could also be rendered, "*Because* he was in the form of God," and that this in fact represents Paul's underlying theology at this point. In other words, when Christ emptied himself he was not divesting himself of deity, but was rather expressing the divine nature, which is self-giving to the core. Here we find a contrast between what has often been thought of as "normal divinity," or God conceived after the pattern of self-serving, power-hungry rulers as would have been normal in the Roman Empire, and the nature of God as revealed in the suffering, servant love of the Messiah Jesus. Gorman, *Inhabiting the Cruciform God*, 9–39.

Though voice in triune harmony sublime,
Laid down his right to sing that mighty chord.

Life beyond created light poured out;
King of kings now servant to the slave;
Now flesh with all flesh destined for the grave;
Now lamb to slaughter led without a shout.

But death cannot contain such boundless love.
God grasped the depths and raised to heaven's height
The Son whose strength was love; whose mercy, might.
The songless one is sung by hosts above!

His name be sung by every bended knee,
His name be sung by every seraph bright,
His name be sung within the darkest night,
And Christ be Lord of glory over me.

So may your mind be that of Christ the Lord,
Who humbly stooped to enter time and space,
Who on the cross in sorrow and disgrace
Sang loud the Triune song—that mighty chord!

5

With Fear and Trembling
The Christ-Shaped Life as Sacrificial Work for the Gospel

PHILIPPIANS 2:12-30

Therefore, you whom I love and who have always been obedient, not only in my presence but now even more in my absence, work out your salvation with fear and trembling, for God is working in you so that you will desire what he has purposed for you—and moreover, that you will accomplish it.

Do everything without grumbling and arguing, so that you may become blameless and innocent, true children of God without fault among a crooked and depraved generation, shining like stars in the universe, holding fast to the word of life. Then I will be able to boast on the day of Christ that in my work for you I did not run in vain. But even if I am poured out like a sacrificial drink offering in service for your faith, I rejoice—and rejoice with all of you. May you also rejoice with me.

But I hope in the Lord Jesus Christ to send Timothy to you soon, so that I might be encouraged in learning how you are doing. I have no one else like him, who will be truly like-minded in concern for you. For everyone is preoccupied with themselves rather than with Jesus Christ. But you know Timothy's character; that he has served with me in the gospel like a child with his father. Therefore I hope to send him immediately to see you on my behalf. And I am convinced in the Lord that I myself will be able to come soon.

In the meantime, I have thought it necessary to send Epaphroditus to you. He is a brother, fellow worker, and fellow soldier to me, and also your messenger and servant. He is longing for you all, and is distressed because you heard that he was sick. For indeed he was sick almost to the point of death, but God had mercy on him—and not on him alone, but also on me, to spare me great sorrow. Therefore I was eager to send him so that you may rejoice as you see him again, and so that I might be free from anxiety. So welcome him in the Lord with joy, and honor those who are like him, for he came near death in his work for Christ, risking his life so that he might help me on your behalf.

ON THE WORKING OUT OF SALVATION

"WORK OUT YOUR SALVATION with fear and trembling." It seems an odd phrase to us. It also seems to be almost contradicted by the phrase which follows: "For God is working in you." But at this point in our reading of Philippians, we are well equipped to see what Paul means. Not only that, but Paul is eager to give us a few more examples of people who embody that idea; namely, Timothy and Epaphroditus.

To once again take in the larger picture, we remember that in this letter Paul is repeatedly sketching a portrait of what we have called the Christ-shaped life. First that portrait was sketched in Paul's description of his own situation of suffering for the sake of the gospel. Then he explained how his audience, the Philippians, are themselves also exemplars of that pattern of life in their partnership with his ministry. Then Paul turns to the supreme example of Christ-shaped life, which is, of course, Christ himself in his incarnation, servant ministry, death, resurrection, and glorification. Now Paul points to a few more exemplars of the gospel embodied in human life and service: his coworkers Timothy and Epaphroditus.

But before he does that, he writes that interesting line about working out one's salvation with fear and trembling, because God is the one working in us. And situated here as it is amid all these exemplars of the Christ-shaped life, we can see rather naturally what Paul means. Salvation here is neither a passive status nor an inert object. It is rather a dynamic act of the living God, an act which is accomplished by his power and grace alone, but which is also inhabited and incarnated by those people who live in union with Christ by faith. Or to put it differently, salvation has already been fully worked for us by God in Christ, and yet it still needs to be "worked out" in the context of our daily lives. Salvation is a gift which God has given to us once-for-all, yet it is the sort of gift which must be unwrapped anew each day and put to work for God's great kingdom purposes.

If it's not too poor an analogy for the grace of God, think about a father giving his son the gift of a new car. The car belongs to the son, free and clear. He doesn't have to work for it. But it's his responsibility and joy to get behind the wheel and drive it every day, as he goes about the tasks that this wonderful machine empowers him to do.

In a similar way, working out our salvation means actively embracing and living out the gift which God has freely given us: an identity, destiny, and purpose which is defined by our union with and likeness to Christ. To work out our salvation means, in short, to joyfully inhabit the Christ-shaped life God has given to us, all in the context of this present world. (Or, to get ahead of ourselves, to "Take hold of that for which Christ took hold of us.")

As we consider these things, we can't help but return to the message of our opening passage; particularly concerning our conformity to God's desires. Here the importance of *desire* once again emerges in verse 13: "*For God is working in you so that you will desire what he has purposed for you—and moreover, that you will accomplish it.*" To work out our salvation means to participate in the work of God which is already guaranteed on the basis of the finished work of Christ, but which is still taking shape in our lives. God has already established his great purpose for us. He is working in our hearts so that we will grow in the grace of agreeing with him in longing for the destiny to which he has called us, and that in this shared desire, our thoughts, words, and actions will actually, and increasingly each day, manifest the purposes of God.

This may be a difficult process. As we have already seen in Philippians, it is not without suffering and sacrifice, for these are in fact characteristic markers of the Christ-shaped life. Perhaps that is why working out or enacting the meaning of our salvation is something to be done "with fear and trembling." It is a reality lived in view of perilous possibilities. The journey toward our Christ-shaped destiny is not to be taken lightly. When we view clearly both the cosmic significance of God's calling, and the crosses we bear along the way, there will indeed be fear and trembling.

Indeed, can there be any true growth toward Christian maturity without fear and trembling? The Psalms and Proverbs repeatedly claim that becoming a wise person (that is, someone whose mind and whose life is in alignment with God and with the world as God designed it) begins with the fear of the Lord. Such fear does not necessarily mean terror that God will smite us. But we should not forget that everyone in the Bible who encountered God did in fact experience literal fear and trembling—not simply respect, but fearful awe before the splendid and terrifying holiness of God. Even the disciples experienced great fear in the presence of Jesus at those moments when they saw him clearly for who he was (such

as in the boat after he calmed the storm, or during his transfigura-
tion.) If we really want to know God, to experience him, to be close
to him—and we understand what we mean by those things—we
should expect to experience some fear and trembling.

And yet simultaneously, this pilgrimage toward Christlikeness and closeness with God is abundantly joyful. It is not, according to Paul, accompanied by "grumbling and arguing." What,
indeed, should be more joyful than walking with our savior toward
the goal which he has earned for us—indeed, the destination for
which we were created? The business of working out our salvation
is a joyous thing, though also of towering significance: not to be
grumbled at, but celebrated and marveled as a priceless gift.

The gift and the task is a life together which Paul can describe
this way: "*Blameless and innocent, true children of God without
fault among a crooked and depraved generation, shining like stars
in the universe, holding fast to the word of life.*" That is Paul's vision
for the life of the church. The words "blameless," "innocent," and
"without fault" might take us off guard—indeed, they may induce
more fear and trembling on our part! We're used to thinking of the
Christian life in terms of God's grace, not human performance.
(Or at least we ought to be. Do we ever grow beyond the dangerous lure of legalism?) However, a careful reading of the New Testament will show that we as modern Christians have sometimes
introduced a false dichotomy between grace and righteous living
which is foreign to the text itself. Of course, we cannot earn our
way into God's favor by our own righteousness. His favor is a gift
which comes purely of his grace. But righteousness is indeed part
of the gift. The goal and outcome of God's grace really is a transformed people; a people who are growing in likeness to the savior
by whose righteousness they are saved. If there is not ultimately
some contrast and distinction between the norms of the world and
the norms of the people of God, and some growing resemblance
between these people and their savior, then the gospel of which the
New Testament speaks is a sham. Saved by God's mercy through
Christ alone, God's people are sinners stepping and stumbling
along a path which leads to glory. Despite our fallenness and our

feebleness, God's work for us and in us really does result in a divine masterpiece which shines forth his glory before a watching world. That is what Paul means when he calls his audience to shine like stars in the universe.[1] It means becoming a living display of the grace and glory of God, and that is something accomplished uniquely through the lives of redeemed sinners.

God's goal, according to Paul, is to create that kind of life in and among human persons, and that is therefore Paul's goal too. When there are such people—flesh and blood people, living in cities like Philippi and gathering there in a local church—who glorify God by being formed after the likeness of his son, that will be something for the apostle to boast about. Not, of course, because he has created it, but because he has, as a vessel of God's grace, witnessed and even participated in the Spirit-empowered work of God. For Paul, that is work worth joining. It is worthy of any sacrifice and suffering it might entail. But such work is, as nothing else is, worthy of our deepest rejoicing, for it is the work in which God accomplishes his creation-purpose of forming a people who inhabit his Christ-shaped love.

THE CHRIST-SHAPED LIFE IS ENACTED AMID THE ORDINARY

The people to whom Paul writes are called to shine like stars in the heavens. Not only are they called, they are promised. This calling-promise of the Christian life is something of cosmic significance. And yet it is enacted by ordinary people in humble circumstances; people with ordinary names, ordinary faces, and ordinary jobs. They are humble servants of an extraordinary savior.

---

1. It is also possible that Paul is alluding here to the great promise given to Abraham in Genesis 15:5, in which God tells him to look up at the stars and to try to count them, saying to him, "So shall your offspring be." This promise was given to further the one given to him already in chapter 12 that "all peoples on earth will be blessed through you." In the New Testament, we are told by Paul that the offspring of Abraham are not only his physical flesh and blood, but also those who share his faith. All believers in Christ are members of this family of faith who shine forth the glory and faithfulness of God to all nations.

The two names which emerge as cases in point are *Timothy* and *Epaphroditus*. In this passage, Paul quickly and rather naturally moves from exalted language about how God's people are to shine like stars in the universe, to some rather mundane travel plans. But for the Christian, there is nothing uncomely about this conjunction, for the intention of God is for his glory to inhabit the mundane—indeed, to glorify every mundane thing under heaven. Timothy and Epaphroditus, in their relationships to Paul and to the Philippians, give us a glimpse of how simple servants, such as you and I may become, can serve this purpose.

Paul writes of Timothy, "*I have no one else like him, who will be truly like-minded in concern for you. For everyone is preoccupied with themselves rather than with Jesus Christ. But you know Timothy's character; that he has served with me in the gospel like a child with his father.*" There are a number of things to note here about Timothy's character. First, he is "like-minded in concern" with Paul for the Philippians. He shares Paul's purposes and affections for God's people. Not only does he have a spirit of fellowship with Paul and his ministry, and not only is his heart directed with him toward service for God's people. These postures of his heart have their basis in his fundamental dedication to Jesus Christ. Timothy "has served with [Paul] in the gospel like a child with his father," but this service is not motivated by a childlike obedience to an earthly authority figure. It is rather an implication of the fact that he has put Christ first in all things. This is what enables him to practice commendable service in partnership with Paul for the sake of the gospel and God's redeemed people. He is, as it were, "preoccupied" with Christ.

How can we carry out our jobs, family responsibilities, and other daily tasks in such a way that we are, at the same time, preoccupied with Christ? The answer—or at least part of it—is implied in Paul's language about sharing the same mind of concern for others. This is a Christian like-mindedness, or perhaps we could better say, a cruciform like-mindedness: a sharing of the mind of the Christ who died for us. The anthem of Paul's life was the re-enactment of the cross in his daily life for the sake of the gospel, so that God's church would be built among the nations and her savior glorified. That is evidenced in all Paul's writings, and certainly in Philippians, not least this very passage: *"But even if I am poured out like a sacrificial drink offering in service for your faith, I rejoice—and rejoice with all of you. May you also rejoice with me."* That kind of cruciform love, shared by Paul, and Timothy, and the church, is a sharing in the very life and heartbeat of the slain Christ and the living God; the eternal song of the blessed Trinity. And it is a life which God's people can inhabit and reenact through any little thing they do.

This is not an occasion for fussing over methods. The thing to understand is that it has already been accomplished in Christ. Insofar as we believe, we are already participants in the cross and the life of divine love. The question is whether we are willing to view all our activities and responsibilities in light of this reality; this truth which is the proper criterion and judge of all our beliefs and actions. The cross of Christ has both crucified and embraced the whole world, and therefore it crucifies and embraces every aspect of our life. We will see it this way if we simply give the time and attention needed to do so.

And of course, it involves commitment; real unflinching commitment to service for the good of others and the furtherance of the gospel. We see this in Paul's unquenchable ministry endurance, and in Timothy, who shared Paul's mind of deep concern for the Philippians. We also see this in the empathy and compassion of Epaphroditus.

Paul describes how Epaphroditus *"is longing for you all, and is distressed because you heard he was sick."* We don't know the exact nature of his illness, but Paul says that he nearly died. Paul also says that *"he came near death in his work for Christ, risking his life so that he might help me on your behalf."* In this way, Epaphroditus is clearly another exemplar of the Christ-shaped life. Like Paul, Timothy, and prospectively the Philippian church, he has embraced the cruciform path of life through sacrificial, loving service on behalf of others, all for the glory of God and the gospel of grace.

But Epaphroditus is also exemplary in this way: he expresses a moving degree of empathy and compassion for God's people, being distressed even to think about other people worrying on his behalf. He is eager to assure the Philippians that he is well, because he wants them to be spared of worry and grief. Being concerned about the emotional wellbeing of others might seem like a simple little thing, but it is a sign of a Christ-shaped heart. To be "preoccupied with Christ" calls us to care deeply about the people around us, even caring about their feelings. The stoic, toughminded attitude which says, "I'll do what I think I should do, your feelings be damned," might be useful in certain kinds of contexts, but it doesn't fit well in the Christian life. We should indeed do what we understand to be right with absolute devotion to Jesus Christ, and we should avoid succumbing to emotional manipulations toward compromise. But even as we practice Christian toughmindedness for the gospel, it should never be divorced from Christian tenderheartedness, which, properly aligned, is an expression of the love of Christ. The goal of the Christian life is not to avoid hurting people's feelings at all costs, yet the feelings of others should still matter to us. An attitude of self-righteous indifference to the emotional wellbeing of others clearly puts us at a distance from the kind of life Christ wants to form in us.[2]

VOCATION DEFINED BY SERVICE

There is a further practical implication of all this for our Christian understanding of calling or vocation. There is a popular idea among Christians that every individual is called to do a very

---

2. Perhaps the feelings of others matter less than the truth, but they should matter a good deal more to us than our own desires to win verbal boxing matches and the justification of our treasured assumptions. When we say, "the truth matters more than your feelings," is it ever the case that we really mean, "my feelings of rightness matter more than your feelings of injury at my words against you"? Jesus was never one to back down from proclaiming uncomfortable truths. Yet could such thinking, which uses the language of truth to prop up my own fragile ego at the expense of my neighbor's heart, be any further from the mind of Christ?

specific thing, and we are to identify this thing by deciding what gives us the most personal excitement, or in which way we are uniquely skilled. Often we call it a "passion." What this means, in effect, is that there is a particular kind of activity, project, goal, or line of work, which we especially want to do, and we think that the meaning of our life is to try our best to do it.

Now, there may not be anything necessarily wrong with this line of thinking. There is nothing wrong in the least with following desires that we believe are God-given and are God-glorifying. The problem lies in the methodology, which I suspect is a bit too influenced by the popular psychology of self-actualization. When we bring this into our thinking about our calling or vocation in life, we can too easily become self-centered instead of God-centered. In the name of serving others, we really seek to serve ourselves by achieving for ourselves something we happen to find personally significant. The agenda for our lives becomes the achievement of something for ourselves, rather than simply loving and obeying God by serving others.

The point is most easily made through practical questions. Perhaps, as we set a course for our lives or face challenging decisions, the most important questions to ask are not, "What is my passion? What is it that I am most gifted at that I should try to do?" But rather: "What needs are there in the world around me? What opportunities lie before me to meet those needs? In which ways do I have the ability to help?" This does not mean that we no longer consider our gifts or desires, but rather that they come second instead of first. We do not ask first, "What will make me happy and fulfilled?" But rather simply seek to obey God by saying "yes" to him at those points of convergence between our abilities, our opportunities, and the needs of others. Here we are able to experience the paradox of happiness: that it is not found by seeking it for ourselves, but in seeking the glory of God and the good of others. After simply obeying God and using our abilities in whatever way (however humble) they are useful for his purposes, we are likely to discover great happiness, passion, and fulfillment in places we may not have expected.

All of this is rooted in the truths we have been contemplating from the beginning of Philippians: the Christ-shaped life, which alone is the truly good and happy one, is formed partly by having our desires pulled back into their God-glorifying form. The Christian life is the marvelous (though sometimes painful) adventure of learning to be supremely happy in God. When we direct our lives toward the practical good of those around us for the sake of God rather than toward some high pinnacle of personal fulfillment, we can know that we are enrolling in the school of Christ-shaped desire, which is also where we will learn the most profound happiness: participatory delight in the glory of God.

WITH FEAR AND TREMBLING

Again, such a life is one which Paul describes as one lived "with fear and trembling." Perhaps it still seems like an odd phrase. But a closer look at Paul's usage of this phrase elsewhere in his writings is illuminating. In 1 Corinthians 2:3, Paul describes how when he first presented himself to the Corinthians, he came to them "with fear and trembling" rather than with a display of wise and persuasive words. His "fear and trembling" seems to imply a posture of humility, partly before his audience, but perhaps even more so before the crucified Christ who was the sole subject of his preaching. We find a similar use of the phrase in 2 Corinthians 7:15, in which Paul commends his audience in part for receiving Titus obediently and "with fear and trembling." The wider context for this meeting had to do with Paul's sending of a strongly worded letter which led the Corinthian church to repentance. But in any case, we see in these personal usages of the phrase "fear and trembling" a strong sense of interpersonal humility, servitude, and obedience—precisely the sort which models the ultimate servant Jesus Christ, who certainly went to the cross with fear and trembling of his own. The picture, then, is not of timidly cowering before God or a human superior, but rather humbly laying ourselves at the feet of others, in the manner of a servant, and with a posture of sacrificial, self-giving love. So considered, Paul's use of the phrase here in Philippians doesn't seem odd at all. It expresses the heart of his message. The courage and confidence of the Christian is found, paradoxically, in the fear and trembling of a humble servant. Cruciformity is the means by which God works his glorious things in, for, and among us.

This is a truth which must permeate the whole structure of our ordinary lives. No responsibility is so great that it cannot be done with self-effacing servitude; no task is so small that it cannot be transfigured by the glory of the Servant King. God in Christ has given us the salvation which is our life. Servant love for the good of those around us, in all activities great and small, is the heartbeat which manifests its presence. Such service for others, done in the power of the crucified and resurrected Christ, is the light which shines in a dark world. In all its simplicity, it is not only a crucial matter of our spiritual formation, but part of God's strategy against the powers of evil. And not only is it a means to such great ends: the cruciform life of self-giving love may well be the purpose for which God created the entire universe.

> *Lord, you have given the world the light of Christ,*
> *The light of servant love.*
> *May it shine in me!*
>
> *May it shine in the thoughts of my mind,*
> *May it shine in the meditations of my heart.*
> *May it shine in the works of my hands,*
> *May it shine in the words of my mouth.*
> *May it shine in all the hours of my day,*
> *May it shine in all the years of my life.*
> *May it shine in the quiet of my solitude,*
> *May it shine in the songs of my fellowship.*
> *May it shine in the darkness of my deepest sadness,*
> *May it shine in the brilliance of my highest joy.*
>
> *Lord, you have given the world the light of Christ,*
> *The light of servant love.*
> *May it shine in me!*

6

For Which Christ Took Hold of Me
The Christ-Shaped Life as Participation in Christ's Death and Resurrection

PHILIPPIANS 3:1-14

*Finally, brothers and sisters, rejoice in the Lord. It is no trouble
for me to repeat myself, and it is a needed reminder for you.*

*Be on your guard against those "dogs" who do evil and
who mutilate the flesh through falsely imposed circumcision.
For it is we who are the true circumcision. We who worship
in the Spirit of God and glory in Christ Jesus do not place our
confidence in the flesh—even though I myself could claim
reasons for such confidence. If anyone has a right to boast
about things of the flesh, I have more: I, circumcised on the
eighth day, was born a true Israelite of the tribe of Benjamin,
as Hebrew as they come! I was an expert in the law as a
Pharisee, zealous in persecuting the church, and immaculate
in my law-keeping.*

But whatever advantage such things were, I have now written them all off as a loss because of Christ. Not just that, I consider all things a loss in light of the all-surpassing value of knowing Christ Jesus my Lord. For his sake I have suffered the loss of all things and considered them as filthy garbage, that I may have Christ and be found in him. In this, I have no righteousness of my own through the law, but a righteousness which comes through the faithfulness of Christ; a righteousness from God which is by faith. So it is that I may know him, as I know the power of his resurrection and share in the fellowship of his sufferings, even being conformed to his death so that I might attain the resurrection from the dead.

I have not yet attained this; I have not yet arrived at my destination. But I press on to take hold of that for which Christ has taken hold of me. Brothers and sisters, I know I have not grasped hold of it yet, but one thing I do: I forget what is behind and reach forward to what lies ahead, pressing on toward the goal, the prize for which God has called me on the upward path in Christ Jesus.

TWO HEARTS, ONE HEARTBEAT

IT IS POSSIBLE TO turn a corner and suddenly find yourself back in the same place you recently left. It happens sometimes to those who are lost—but also those who have just been found. This seems to be what is happening in Paul's discourse at the beginning of chapter 3. After his pleasant reminder to rejoice in the Lord, Paul's words are jarring: "Watch out for those dogs!" (A term of contempt.) And yet, despite this sudden acridity in Paul's otherwise jubilant letter, we soon see that he is in fact returning to the same joyful theme: the infinite worth of the Christ-shaped life, in which we have been included through our union with the death and resurrection of Jesus Christ. Paul once was lost amid all the valuables of a distinguished life. He has now been found in the all-surpassing value of knowing Christ—and once again, his discourse finds itself in the heartbeat of cruciform joy.

As we place this passage in the structure of Philippians, we could say that this epistle is a creature with a single heartbeat but two hearts. The heartbeat—to say it again—is the joy which is found in the pursuit of the Christ-shaped life; a life of humility, self-giving love, and service destined for the glory of God. The first "theological heart" of the letter is 2:5–11, in which we see the incarnation, servitude, death, resurrection, and glorification of Jesus Christ sketched as the pattern (and in fact the foundation) of the Christian life. Jesus exemplified both the character of God and the character of those recreated in his image. The present passage (3:1–14) is the second theological heart of Philippians. Paul's message here refers to the same great reality, but shows in more detail our human connection to it; namely participation in the death and resurrection of Christ through faith. Here Paul goes beyond calling us to imitate Christ and declares that Christianity means actual inclusion in the Christ event. Paul continues to sing the song of Christ crucified and glorified—the mighty chord of Triune love—but now transposed into a different key.

THE ISSUE OF CIRCUMCISION

But the backdrop for Paul's joyful gospel message—and indeed the backdrop of his joyful Christian life—is a darker story. There is good news because it is spoken against the bad news. The children can only be found if they once were lost. The light shines because it pierces the darkness. The story of Paul's life is an explosion of new life and joy, but to say this implies a contrast with a former state of death and sorrow. Or as Paul himself might have put it with regard to his message in this passage, there can only be a resurrection if there is first a cross. Here Paul describes the story of his life in a world which has now been crucified to him. The "dogs" or the circumcisers are those who, far from participating in the cruciform life of Christ, are participants in the world which crucified him; the world which has been conquered by the cross and the resurrection.

Circumcision hardly seems like such a matter of life-and-death to us now. But for the Israelites, it was a fundamental marker of personal, religious, and national identity going all the way back to Abraham. Circumcision was a marker of the true people of God; those who were the offspring of God's chosen servant Abraham. So it was for thousands of years.

But in the first century AD, a startling and exciting message began to spread throughout Israel and around the world: that through the death and resurrection of the Messiah Jesus, the God of Israel had proven himself to be the creator-redeemer of all things and the king over all nations, and that any person, whatever their tribe, tongue, or nationality, could be a member of his covenant people if they simply joined themselves to this Jesus in faith and allegiance by being baptized into the community of belief. This is the message of the New Testament; the good news of the kingdom of God preached and enacted by Jesus himself, and later proclaimed and explained by Paul and other apostles to the nations. This was genuinely good news; something to be joyfully proclaimed and jubilantly celebrated, for it was and remains simply the message that in a world where so much has gone wrong, there is a good creator God who loves his people and is calling them back to himself to participate in the restoration of all things. It is the good news that all nations, Jews and gentiles, Greeks and Romans, Asians, Africans, Europeans, Native Americans, Pacific Islanders, and every tribe and tongue of people under the sun, have been invited to become the covenant people of God: the celebrants and sharers of his redeeming love.

The circumcision issue to which Paul alludes stands at the center of all of this. The true people of God are not defined by circumcision, says Paul, but by the Holy Spirit in whom they are joined to Jesus Christ and by whom they worship the creator of all. Those who insist on circumcision have denied the gospel—the good news that God in Christ has thrown open the doors of his covenant to people of every tribe, tongue, and nation. They are trying to nail shut a door which God himself has opened. They are, Paul suggests, clinging to a theology of the flesh; a theology of pride and pedigree; a theology of ethnic exclusion and entitlement; a theology of pious law-keeping; a theology of human glory rather than of God's grace.[1]

This is where Paul becomes autobiographical. He too once lived by this theology of human pride and pedigree—and what a pedigree he had! *"I, circumcised on the eighth day, was born a true Israelite of the tribe of Benjamin, as Hebrew as they come! I was an expert in the law as a Pharisee, zealous in persecuting the church, and immaculate in my law-keeping."* But the gospel interrupted Paul's life even as it had invaded the world—with a militant love. Paul's conversion, like all conversions, was an exchange of stories. He jumped ship mid-course, from a previous journey marked by zealous pride in his religious-national identity, and into a journey marked out by the crucified Christ; a journey whose destination is a resurrected fellowship of peoples of all nations. Paul's old story, with all its achievements and accolades, is no longer important to him. Not that there was anything at all wrong with being a Hebrew and a Benjamite, with being circumcised, or indeed with being a Pharisee[2] (of course, being such was no good reason for him to persecute Christians). But for Paul, only one thing really matters: to be united with the crucified and resurrected Christ; to be drawn into his story and therefore to share in his redeeming victory over

---

1. The Protestant reformer Martin Luther famously rooted much of his theology in a distinction between what he called a theology of glory and a theology of the cross. This Lutheran distinction expresses very well the meaning of this passage in Philippians, which contrasts the way of human glory, pride, and exclusion which was sometimes expressed through circumcision and law-keeping, and the way of faith, humility, and inclusion which is established by the cross of Jesus Christ.

2. The Pharisees are often typecast as villains in the gospels, since more often than not they are the target of Jesus's most stinging rebukes. However, we should not automatically read the word "Pharisee" to mean "wicked, self-righteous legalist." Remember that Nicodemus and Joseph of Arimathea were both members of the Pharisaical circle, yet both are remembered as people who responded believingly and honorably to Jesus.

all things. That is the path onto which Paul has stepped. That is the destiny which is now his consuming goal.

THAT FOR WHICH CHRIST TOOK HOLD OF ME

That is why Paul, in his deliciously rich phrase, strives to take hold of that for which Christ took hold of him.[3] The significant things of his old life are no longer significant to him, for he has now grasped the purpose for which he has been redeemed—and therefore, we may infer, the purpose for which he was created in the first place. He has, in Christ, stepped back into the trajectory of his God-given destiny.

Here we are reminded of a few concepts which figured significantly in previous chapters. We think back to chapter 1, in which we considered the concept of destiny as a story or trajectory in life which is created for us by the purpose and power of God—a new path with a certain outcome, onto which we may step through faith. We also noticed Paul's emphasis on the attunement of our desires so that they are rightly aligned with the heart of God and with the destiny he has given us. This is a matter of agreeing with God in our pursuits and desires; of realigning our value system so that we are no longer driven through life by the kinds of accomplishments which marked Paul's old life, but rather see the purpose of our lives in light of the Christ-shaped life which is the source and goal of Christian existence.

We are also reminded of Paul's interesting phrase from chapter 2: "Work out your salvation with fear and trembling, for God is working in you." To "Take hold of that for which Christ took hold of me" has a similar kind of duality to it. God in Christ has already

3. We might perhaps observe that in Paul's language of "taking hold," he is possibly paralleling the language of "grasping" equality with God which he invoked in 2:6. Christ did not grasp after the prestige of the heavenly throne; instead he became the hand of the Father reaching down to grasp his wounded world and raise it into his life of self-giving love. This is that for which Christ has "grasped" or "taken hold" of us. Similarly, we must not "grasp" after the honors bestowed by the world, but rather join God's hand in holding fast to the cruciform love and resurrected life in Christ.

accomplished the definitive act of "taking hold." He has already grasped our hand, but it remains for us to grasp his in return. God has already given us our path and promised his guiding presence; it remains for us to take his hand and walk with him by faith.

In other words, "To take hold of that for which Christ took hold of me" is a calling which is already a promise from God, yet one which demands real striving and "taking hold" on our part. As Paul illustrates, this process is not without a sense of loss and sacrifice. Paul had to say goodbye to his old life and all the bragging rights which were attached to it. There is a resonance here with many things Jesus himself said. "Whoever would be my disciple must lay down his life, take up his cross, and follow me." "Whoever wants to save his life will lose it, but whoever loses his life for me will save it."

But whatever must be sacrificed in pursuit of the Christ-shaped life is, according to Paul, not truly worthy of value in the first place. To state this inversely, all things truly worth having are already present in Christ, for he is the very paradigm of the old creation's purpose, and the prototype of the new creation's goal. Anything good given up in pursuit of our Christ-given destiny is something which will be given back to us, resurrected and transfigured into its most God-glorifying form.

TO KNOW CHRIST IS TO ENTER A NEW WORLD

But we have not yet come to the heart of the matter. We have spoken of what Paul has given up, but not what he has received. We considered, albeit briefly, the old life which we must lay down, but not the nature of the new life which we must take up. What exactly is "that for which Christ took hold of me?"

Paul tells us rather directly: "*I consider all things a loss in light of the all-surpassing value of knowing Christ Jesus my Lord, that I may have Christ and be found in him.*" Paul goes on to describe this new life of knowing Christ in terms of receiving his righteousness, "*a righteousness which comes through the faithfulness of Christ.*" He says that this all pulls in the direction of knowing "*the power of his resurrection and [sharing] in the fellowship of his sufferings, even being conformed to his death so that I might attain the resurrection from the dead."*

Paul's answer then, in brief, is to "know Christ." That is a phrase which rolls easily off evangelical tongues, but what does Paul mean by knowing Christ? In this passage, he connects it with two words inseparably bound together in the gospel: *righteousness* and *resurrection*. These two together, as finished accomplishments of Jesus Christ, describe the future goal which defines and animates our present faith. As Christians, we are people who inhabit Christ's righteousness (which is the very faithfulness and goodness of God) and his resurrection life (which, more than a mere resuscitated individual heartbeat, means a new world created by the victory of God over sin, death, and the powers of the age). It's worth taking a moment to unpack these words just a bit further.

Righteousness

Paul says that he has no righteousness of his own, but rather a righteousness which comes through Christ. There's a scholarly dispute on translation here which cannot be easily avoided.[4] Some translations read that that the righteousness comes through *faith in Christ*, while others say that it comes through *the faithfulness of Christ*. These are alternate ways of translating the Greek phrase *pistis Christou*. The grammar of this phrase is famously ambiguous. First, the word *pistis* can be translated as either "faith" or "faithfulness." These have quite a different sense in English, but both senses can be found in the Greek *pistis*. The Greek language of Paul's time—and arguably Paul's theology—did not always make a clear-cut distinction between faith as personal trust/confidence and as loyalty/allegiance. To make matters more complex, the preposition in the phrase is ambiguous: should it be read as "faithfulness *of* Christ," or "faith *in* Christ?" *Christou* is the genitive form of *Christ*, and Greek genitives are often highly flexible in terms of what kind

4. If you'd rather not bother with some Greek technicalities, feel free to skip the rest of this paragraph.

of preposition or relation is implied. The practical question is whether Paul is talking about his righteousness as deriving from the faith which he has placed in Christ, or from the faithfulness of Christ himself.

We could spend ages trying to figure this out, and scholars have spilled much ink discussing it. However, when we read the phrase in context, I would suggest that such wrangling misses the point, since both meanings are necessarily being invoked throughout this passage. Immediately after Paul says that he has *"a righteousness which comes through the faithfulness of Christ"* (or *faith in Christ*), he specifies that this is *"a righteousness which is from God which is by faith."* It is clear either way that personal faith is involved. We can see this in the broader context, too. Paul has already emphasized that he no longer places personal confidence in his religious pedigree—his confidence (or faith) is now in Christ. And yet the object of this faith, however we read the Greek grammar, is clearly Jesus Christ; namely his death and resurrection, which Christ has accomplished for him and in which he participates. Taken as a whole, this passage emphasizes both personal faith in Christ, and the way in which such faith means personal involvement in the faithful, righteous work of Christ which was accomplished through the cross and the resurrection.

The important thing here is that this passage gives us a wonderfully enlarged vision of the meaning of *righteousness.* Righteousness means the faithfulness of God which has come to us in Christ. This is something much bigger than what might immediately come to mind when we think of righteousness. We might think of righteousness merely in terms of personal moralism; as good behavior of which God approves. We may also, especially as protestants, emphasize righteousness as a salvific status or gift of grace which has been conferred upon us by God through Christ. Both of these are true enough. It is important to remember that God's people have been entrusted with important moral responsibilities, and even more important to remember that we do not attain God's grace through such moral effort but only by God's gift. But the biblical sense of receiving God's righteousness, while including these ideas, points to something much bigger than our personal, individual status. It ultimately means receiving a kingdom; inhabiting the realm of God's goodness, wisdom, and love by faith in Christ. Receiving God's righteousness through faith means, in other words, to step into the new world which God has created in Christ, in which all his good, wise, and loving purposes for creation are fulfilled. That surely involves a personal trust in God's grace, alone by which this gift is received, and it must surely lead toward a transformed life of the sort which is fitting for citizens of the kingdom. But God's righteousness which is given to us is so much more than something merely personal or individual. It is a whole new (or better, renewed) universe in which we now live through our union with Christ.

Resurrection

The other main concept to which "knowing Christ" is attached in this passage is *resurrection*. Paul writes, "*So it is that I may know him, as I know the power of his resurrection and share in the fellowship of his sufferings, even being conformed to his death so that I might attain the resurrection from the dead.*" To know Christ means not only to receive his righteousness and therefore enter the realm of God's goodness which has been inaugurated by his ministry, but also relatedly, to participate in his resurrection. As with the word *righteousness, resurrection* means more than first meets the eye. Resurrection does not merely mean a restored heartbeat, but a whole new quality of life which has been defined by the crucified and risen Christ. Nor should we think of the resurrection as merely referring to an eternal heavenly afterlife, but rather as participation in a whole new creation which fulfills all the creator's good purposes for this world.

But of course (the careful reader wonders if I have gotten ahead of myself), a cross comes first. Paul's words establish an unbreakable link between sharing in the fellowship of Christ's sufferings, being conformed to his death, and sharing in his resurrection. Paul's connecting phrase here is "so that," which indicates that union with Christ in his death is a precondition for union with him in his resurrection. These are two basic facts about Christian faith and life which cannot be separated. Just as we cannot separate the cross from the resurrection in the significance of Jesus's ministry (remove one and the meaning of the other is lost), so we cannot remove either from our definition of the Christian life.

Paul's words suggest that there are at least two aspects of sharing in the death of Christ. They are found in two clauses which are parallel to one another: "*Share in the fellowship of his sufferings,*" and "*being conformed to his death.*" These phrases are almost synonymous with each other, yet each seem to have a different nuance to them. Paul's intent could be to say, in essence, "We do not merely share in Jesus's suffering. Our commitment to him must go the whole way, such that we will even share in his death." But Paul is also presenting a juxtaposition between the idea of *sharing/ fellowship* in Christ's cross, and that of *conformity* to Christ's cross. Again, these ideas are very close to one another. But the difference, perhaps, is that which lies between inhabiting a reality and following an example. Significantly, Paul lists both. The deep connection which has been forged between the believer and the cross of Christ must be understood on two equally important levels: the cross defines the reality in which we live, such that we have entered a deep union with our crucified savior, and the cross is also our supreme pattern of imitation in life. These are not simply two parallel truths of the Christian faith; it is more the case that the first leads to the second. It is because our lives have been grafted into the life of Christ, our sins being crucified in him, that we are then called to take up his cross as the banner of victory in which we live as self-sacrificial servants in his name.

This is the death which leads to resurrection. In his death, Jesus has crucified the old world of sin and death, of human pride and power, and his resurrection has inaugurated the new world of righteousness and life, of divine power and glory. So it is that by having fellowship through faith in the cross of Christ, we die to that old world which held us captive and in which we too raged against God. But having been bound to the cross with Christ, so we also rise with him in his resurrection.[5] Believers in Christ have already been drawn with him into the New Creation; the kingdom of his eternal goodness, wisdom, and love. We are already citizens of his country, even as we still live in the structures of the old world. We are promised that at Christ's return, we will rise and enjoy eternal life with him forever in his fully established kingdom.

But this pattern does not only operate on the level of our spiritual union with Christ or our salvific status. It is a pattern meant to be lived every day. With every rising of the sun, we once again commit to denying ourselves, taking up our crosses, and following Jesus on the Golgotha road. As Paul writes in Galatians 6:14 (he could almost have said it in this passage, with all his renunciation of human boasting), *"May I never boast except in the cross of our Lord Jesus Christ, through which the world has been crucified to me, and I to the world."* But as we embrace the Christ-defined pattern of dying to the world and to ourselves, we embrace the life of abundant joy, grace, and peace which he gives to us through the Spirit.

Dying to Ourselves and Living to God

At this point, we need to ask what exactly it means to die to ourselves and to participate in the death of Christ, seeing as it is the precursor to sharing in his resurrection. This is near to the heart of what Christian faith is all about, but I think that sometimes we get it wrong. There is often a great emphasis put on the importance of dying to ourselves, but it often seems as though this is taken to mean something akin to self-hatred, or at the very least self-deprecation. Perhaps dying to ourselves means the rejection of the idea that there could be anything good within us, or perhaps the stifling of personal desires. Many of these ideas seem, to me, to go much too far in the direction of rejecting something good which God has made. There is nothing wrong with having a "self." God has created us to have "selves," and he has made nothing evil. In spite of some of our pious habits of the mind, we pay God no honors by

---

5. This is the meaning of Christian baptism, as we see in Romans 6:1–11.

disparaging his handiwork. There are indeed many times in which it is necessary for us, as sinful and prideful creatures, to say with John the Baptist that "He must increase, I must decrease." There are times (indeed, far more often than we may care to admit) in which our sense of selfhood is permeated by an inordinate self-centeredness. But this problem is not addressed by gorging ourselves on thick slices of humble pie. That may even contribute to the problem. Self-deprecation is, after all, simply a negative form of self-preoccupation.

Perhaps the problem is that we have tended to think of dying to ourselves primarily as something negative; as the rejection of self rather than the affirmation of God. The denial of self, while often a needed corrective, is not an intrinsic good. The intrinsic, positive good we are pursuing, rather, is participation in the self-giving, servant love of God which was revealed and enacted in the death and resurrection of Christ. The theologian Emil Brunner said something similar: "But to die with [Christ] means: to devote our lives to the service of others and to sacrifice our pride and self-righteousness by faith in him, who for our sakes had to sacrifice his life on the cross."[6] So perhaps the phrase, "Die to yourself" only gets it half right. Perhaps we would do better to say, "Live to God. Embrace the life of self-giving love which has always been God's nature and which has been richly given to us in the cross of Jesus Christ." When we live to God, there will necessarily be some dying-to-self involved, but death is never an end-in-itself. The end of the matter is being fully alive.

This is all of great importance when pondering the question of what exactly it means to know Christ. According to Paul, the most important thing in his life (and everyone else's) is to know Jesus Christ. As Christians (particularly evangelicals), we tend to place a great deal of emphasis on "knowing God" or a "personal relationship with Jesus Christ." This emphasis is entirely appropriate. But we don't always fully appreciate the depths of what it means. The present passage tells us that this relational knowledge of God goes far beyond emotional, personal experience. It means that our

6. Brunner, *Great Invitation and Other Sermons*, 132.

lives, both individually and corporately as the church, have been fused to the life of Christ, such that in his death we have also died, and in his resurrection we now live. It means that our lives have become embedded in his sacrificial death and therefore also pulled inexorably toward the promise of resurrection. It means that by faith we have been drawn into the realm of God's righteousness which has been given to us in Christ. In short, "knowing Christ" means much more than a personal experience (though it must, of course, become that too). It means that we have entered a whole new world—a world defined by the self-giving, life-creating love of God which has appeared in Jesus Christ.

OLD PATH, NEW PATH

This is the goal for which Paul so ardently strives, struggling in daily life to "take hold of that for which Christ took hold of me." In humility, he assures his audience that he has not yet arrived. God's promised work in him, well underway as it may be, is still incomplete. In response to the fact that Christ has already taken hold of him to draw him into the saving drama of his death and resurrection, Paul is also taking hold of this as his destiny. This is a great both/and of the Christian life: that we take an active role in grasping the identity, destiny, and mission which God has already graciously given us. In other words (Paul's, to be exact), we work out our salvation with fear and trembling, for it is God who works in us to will and act according to his good purpose.

This means that we are on a journey. Like Paul, we have not yet arrived, but we keep striving forward, our eyes fixed on the great Christ-shaped goal which God has placed before us. We have been called onto the upward path, and our daily discipline and delight is to walk it joyfully every day.

Also like Paul, there is a striking contrast between the path we walk now and the path we used to tread. This passage ends with stirring imagery of the Christian life as an upward journey, or perhaps a marathon race. This forms a strong contrast with how the passage began, with Paul's description of his former path. Paul used to walk the road of pride, pedigree, and prestige, but now his feet have been set upon a new path: the way of the cross; the way of knowing Christ and being formed after his pattern of self-sacrificial love; the way of righteousness and resurrection.

All believers in Christ, whether they are still learning to take their first steps or are pilgrims far along the way, share this basic experience. As human beings, we are all born into Adam's fallen race and into a world of estrangement from God. But God in Christ has established a new race and a new world, in which we participate not through privileged position or moral effort, but by grace through faith—the faith which is a participation in the faithfulness of God. We have all been born as members of a company of rebels traveling the road away from their God, but God has given us a new road and made us to be a fellowship of pilgrims traveling the upward path back to his side. The way is long and difficult and there are crosses to be borne. But at the end of the road is resurrection, and Christ is with us every step of the way.

Each day of our journey, we must beware of those things which would cause us to stumble or to stray back onto our old path. Paul insists on looking ahead; he does not longingly gaze back upon his old road of pharisaical ambition. We are with Paul on the new path of the Christ-shaped life, but we must take caution about whatever might pull us back toward our old path. Paul in this passage warns us especially of the dangers of worldly status symbols, whether of a secular or religious nature.

Again, we are confronted with the dynamics of desire. We all have desires for success, for recognition, for the approval and esteem of those whose opinions especially matter to us. We all have dreams of things we'd like to achieve in life. None of this is wrong, so long as these desires are given back to God, who is their first source and final goal. But in this world, there are many possibilities laid out before us of pursuing our goals according to the world's agenda rather than God's. It is possible even for our most pious ambitions to become idols; ways of asserting our identity and significance apart from Jesus Christ. Does our involvement with church activity, or our effort toward deeper knowledge and sanctification, ever become more about proving ourselves to others (or even to ourselves) than about service to others for the sake of Christ? Even the most self-effacing service can be undertaken as an attempt to earn a badge of superiority. Do we not sometimes feel tempted to drape our sacrifices and our sufferings before the eyes of others and to relish the good attentions they bring us? This is the dangerous allure of self-righteousness, when Christlikeness is pursued for purposes other than Christ himself, and when our conspicuous rejection of worldliness becomes utterly worldly. This is where we see the ongoing contrast between the Christ-shaped life and the life of the world. It is a contrast between participation in the kinds of statuses, images, and identities which the world (including the churchly world) celebrates, and participation in the crucified and risen Christ—for no other sake than Christ himself.

CONCLUSION

Here we come to the heart of it all—the heart of the Christian life, and the heart of existence itself. God alone, as known through participation in the death and resurrection of Christ, is the intrinsic and inherently worthy goal of human life. It is this for which Christ took hold of us, and this is what must remain our constant and highest goal.

Some things are good as a means to an end, while others are good as ends-in-themselves. Knowing and loving God through Christ in the fellowship of the Spirit is the only ultimate end-in-itself. The enjoyment of earthly things (contrary to some religious impulses) is a great good, but a secondary one. To make the world a better place is also a great good, but again, it is secondary. Such secondary goods are means (necessary means, to be sure) by which we participate in the great end of all things, which is our relation to God through Christ by the Holy Spirit. The first and final purpose of human existence is to enter the communion of divine love which has been established, revealed, and opened before us in the life, death, and resurrection of Jesus Christ. Anything we can do in this world is significant only insofar as it plays a part in this.

This may sound simple enough, but in our world, it is deeply scandalous—even revolutionary. To highlight the scandal of it in the eyes of modern sensibilities, we might put it this way. In theory, a person who lived in isolation and never accomplished anything toward making the world a better place and yet lived in worshipful communion with God his or her whole life, would have a more fulfilled, purposeful existence than the person who accomplished massive feats for the social good yet did not know God. That perhaps puts it too starkly—the person who lives in worshipful communion with God is certainly drawn into God's mission of love and redemption in the world. According to Philippians, such a person must surely be involved (sacrificially, even) in the work of the gospel. But the final goal of any good activity is that human persons—ourselves and others—might know God through participation in the crucified and resurrected life of Christ. So many of our good endeavors are, to us, little more than distractions from the one truly important thing.

If Paul, the great apostle, could not claim to have arrived yet at this goal, then surely we cannot either. And yet, may his great refrain of purpose resound in every activity of our lives: *"One thing I do: I forget what is behind and reach forward to what lies ahead, pressing on toward the goal, the prize for which God has called me on the upward path in Christ Jesus."* Of course we have not attained this goal yet, but we can live in the light of our destination every day if we live according to the pattern which Christ himself gave us—the pattern of new life which comes from his sacrificial, self-giving love. Every day presents us with countless opportunities to participate in the death and resurrection of Christ. As God's redeemed people, these are the great truths which already define us and mark us as his own, setting us apart from the world's value system and from the old paths we used to tread. We all have a long way to go. But may we realize anew, in all the tasks and challenges which God sets before us, and in all the responsibilities and relationships which he has entrusted to us, the call to joyfully strive toward that for which Christ has taken hold of us: the joy of sacrificial love, the joy of resurrection, the joy of the Christ-shaped life.

O God, you alone are our source, and you alone are our goal. You alone are our beginning and our end, our Alpha and Omega. In you alone we live, in you alone we die. By your Holy Spirit, make our life, in every moment, conform to your Son Jesus. By his death, crucify us to our false desires in this present evil age, and resurrect us into his life of everlasting love. Draw us to you, O Lord; upward and onward to you; ever and always to you. For yours is the kingdom, the power, and the glory. May your name be forever praised! In the Name of the Son and by the power of the Spirit do we pray, Amen.

7

But Our Citizenship Is in Heaven
The Christ-Shaped Life as Embodying the Mind of Christ

PHILIPPIANS 3:15—4:9

Therefore, may all who are mature share this same frame of mind. If anyone thinks differently, God will clear things up for you. In any case, let us live up to what we have already attained.

Brothers and sisters, join together in following my example, as you watch those who walk according to the pattern you have seen in us. For you should know (as I have told you before, and tell you again with tears) that there are many who live otherwise: as enemies of the cross of Christ. Their destiny is destruction, their god is their stomach, and their glory is their shame. Their mind is set on the things of this present realm. But our citizenship is in heaven, and we are eagerly awaiting our savior who is from there: the Lord Jesus Christ. Through the power by which he already rules over and orders all things, he will reorder our lowly bodies after the pattern of his own glorious body. Therefore, brothers and sisters, dear friends whom I love and deeply miss, who are my joy and my crown: stand firm in the Lord!

I plead with Euodia and I plead with Syntyche to have the same mind in the Lord. And I ask that you, my true companion, would help these women, for they have contended side-by-side with me for the cause of the gospel, together with Clement and the rest of my coworkers, whose names are written in the book of life.

May you always rejoice in the Lord. I repeat myself: rejoice! May you be known by all people for your gentleness. The Lord is near: do not be anxious about anything, but in every situation, present your requests to God by prayer and petition, with thanksgiving. Then the peace of God, which is beyond all our understanding, will guard your hearts and minds in Christ Jesus.

Finally, brothers and sisters: whatever is true, whatever is noble, whatever is right, whatever is pure, whatever is lovely, whatever is admirable—if anything is excellent or praiseworthy—set your minds on such things! Whatever you have learned from me, whether by my teaching, my words, or my example, put it into practice. The God of peace will be with you.

LEARNING TO THINK WITH THE MIND
OF HEAVEN

As WE HAVE SEEN repeatedly by now, the book of Philippians is the roadmap for a journey—the joyful pilgrimage which traces the footsteps of our savior. He is the pioneer who has gone before us, establishing the reality in which we live and the destiny which awaits us, and who, by his Spirit, shapes us into conformity with his pattern of death and resurrection; of self-giving love and God-glorifying life. But Jesus is not merely a venerable example from the past who inspires us, nor is he merely a distant sovereign who commands us to journey toward a future goal. He is here in our present, and he is with us every step of the way. In Philippians 4:5, Paul says this with utter simplicity yet fathomless profundity: "*The Lord is near.*" That truth, properly understood, is the sum of all Christian theology and living.[1]

In the previous passage, Paul has given a deep meditation on the meaning of Christian life as participation in the death and resurrection of Jesus, in which, by faith, we are drawn into the righteousness of God. None of us have yet fully arrived at this goal, but all who believe in Christ are already recipients of the great promise—true children of God and co-heirs with Christ. None of us are therefore *mature* in the highest sense of the word. Yet for Paul, Christian maturity means having a basic knowledge of who we are and where we are going—that is, knowing that we are sharers in a reality which has been defined by the cross rather than the value systems of the world, and that the promised goal for which we long is defined by the resurrected life of Christ, rather than the various versions of "the good life" which this world has on offer.

---

1. Here, in short, is what I mean by this claim: simply invoking the title "Lord" should remind us of several Scriptural connections with this title. We are reminded first of all that Jesus is Lord—the true king who reigns over the world and the powers of the age, in contradistinction to the claims of all human kings, emperors, and Caesars. The second connection is more remote in terms of the biblical languages, but also important: that the LORD, YHWH, is the transcendent and holy creator God whose presence is incarnate in the Lord Jesus. In short, the Lord is the holy and sovereign God who created and rules the world. When thinking of God in such terms, it would be natural to think of him as being far removed from our world of sin. Yet the marvelous mystery of the gospel is that in Christ, this high and holy Lord of all has come very near: "The word became flesh and made his dwelling among us." The Lord has come to us, lived among us, died for us, risen for us, and he will dwell with us forever. Therefore the nearness of the Lord is not only the heart of the gospel, but also the heart of the Christian life, in which we return to our creation-purpose of dwelling with God and the community of the redeemed in the renewed earth.

That is why Paul says that those who are mature will take such a view of things. Those who are on their way to maturity will have a sense of where they are going and have a desire to be there. Therefore there is a sense in which the mature will have an awareness of their own immaturity—yet also a confidence in the ground which God has already put under their feet. They will know, in other words, the two things John Newton claimed to know: that they are "great sinners, but Christ is a great savior." They will know that they are not in heaven, but they will also know that in Christ and through the Spirit, a bit of heaven is in them.

This is why, throughout the whole epistle, Paul has a repeated focus on the Christian mind. This is not merely the Christian mind in the intellectual sense of a theology which goes deep and soars high—as excellent as that is. The word *phroneo* (or variations of it) is one Paul uses repeatedly throughout Philippians, and it is translated in terms like "mindset" or "like-minded." This word has the connotation of practical wisdom rather than intellectual theory, although in Paul's usage, the meaning transcends both. We could think of it as a *life-transforming value orientation*. It is an outlook on reality which is shared between persons, first and foremost between Christ himself and the believer, and secondly among the Christian community and all the interpersonal relations it contains. Paul's goal is that Christian believers, whose lives have been enfolded into the crucified and resurrected life of Christ, will also learn to think in a Christ-shaped pattern and with a Christ-saturated imagination. However, such thinking is not to occur merely in the form of individual contemplation. The point is for the believing community to share this mindset together.

To this end, Paul calls attention to his own example. Perhaps this takes us by surprise: has the preacher of humility suddenly begun to toot his own horn? Has the theologian of the cross embraced again the old dead-end theology of human glory—the very kind of prideful path which in the previous passage was considered a pile of garbage?

There is nothing prideful, however, in parents setting an example for their children, nor in a guide setting a course for a group of less experienced hikers. There is nothing improper in the piano teacher telling her student to watch her hands. The point is that following the pilgrimage of the Christ-shaped life is something we do together, and it is a mercy of God that there are some further along the path than us, in whose footsteps we may also tread.

Unfortunately, the power of example can run in more than one direction, and not all of them are good. Paul calls the Philippians to follow his example, not to flaunt his own ego, but to help draw the people he loves further away from the example of those whose lives defy the cross of Christ. Tragically, these people have turned the Christ-shaped life on its head. Perhaps they are the self-same "dogs" about which Paul has already spoken a word of warning. Paul describes their life again in strong language. Their destiny is very different from that which is promised to the Philippian believers. Their god is not the Lord who died for the sake of others; they live to fill their own stomachs. Paul's rhetoric here bristles with irony: "Their glory is their shame." Of course, Paul could well use the same words to describe his own former way of life. All the glories of his old life as a Pharisee have turned out for him to be nothing but shame in light of the all-surpassing gift of knowing Christ. His mind too was set on earthly things before it was overturned by the value system of heaven.

That is Paul's great desire: that the value system of heaven which has invaded the world through Jesus Christ, which has become his value system, will be embraced by all God's people as their way of thought and life. Here he invokes the language of citizenship. The challenge and promise of the Christian life is that we will learn to think, love, and live according to the norms of the country of which we have already been made citizens. Paul's language evokes the tension between the already and not yet: our heavenly citizenship is already a reality, but we are eagerly awaiting our Savior who is already there and will return one day, bringing down to earth with him the realm of which we are already citizens. He already rules over all things, yet we await the day when our whole being, including our bodies, will be remade to fit the realm of his eternal rule.

This has endless implications for the Christian life. All that we are and all that we do has already been established by the gospel of Jesus Christ—our citizenship in heaven is a sheer gift. And yet (this is the paradox of Christian existence) we are called every day to live out the truth of the identity we have been given, and while it is an irrevocable gift, our practice of it is a work in progress. (We again remember Paul's paradoxical instruction to work out our salvation with fear and trembling, because it is God who works in us to will and act according to his good purpose.) The whole of the Christian life is the adventure of learning to live as a member of God's kingdom, even in the midst of this present world. God's children are those who incarnate his good and gracious rule over all things, shining like stars in the sky in the midst of a "warped and crooked generation."

This truth holds great power for our own formation. We are not living the Christian life under the pressure of trying to become something we are not, nor under the pressure (almost as crippling) of trying to become the best version of who we have always been. We are rather becoming that which we already are in Christ, which we have already been recreated to be. We are not living by the anxiety produced by what we are not, nor by the pride of what we think we are, but rather by the unshakable power of promise: the future reality which has already been given to us. We know that we can become like Christ, not by any possibility in ourselves, but by the reality of God's future which has reached into our present and grasped us in an unbreakable love.

Again, the implications are endless. To enact our citizenship means to "stand firm in the Lord." It means that believers in God's church, such as Euodia and Syntyche, should pursue peace in their relationships; the kind of unity which comes from holding in common the self-giving mind of Christ. Such unity must always mark those who work together for the sake of the gospel.

But in this passage, Paul shows a particular concern for how our heavenly citizenship impacts our mindset—our mentality or attitude in the midst of everyday life. Philippians 4:4–9 is a cascading river of words describing the posture of the Christian mind:

Joy. Gentleness. The presence of God. Non-anxiousness. Thanks-giving. Prayer. Peace. Truth. Nobility. Rightness. Purity. Loveli-ness. Admirability. Excellence. Praiseworthiness. We can get lost in the midst of all these words, much as we might get lost in a large garden filled with beautiful plants, trees, and statues. (Getting lost in the midst of the good, the true, and the beautiful is not such a bad thing. Perhaps to be lost in such a place is, in fact, to be found.)

THE JOY OF HEAVEN IS AN ACQUIRED TASTE

But lest we lose our focus entirely, we must remember this, which we have been considering since chapter 1 of Paul's epistle: the call of Christ-shaped destiny is a call toward rightly-ordered desire. It is the call to discern that which is best; that which has true and lasting value, and therefore to hold in our hearts a piece of the future which has already been promised to us. God has already given us heaven. But do we really want it?

I suppose that everybody wants to live forever in paradise—especially considering the more frightening alternatives. But do we truly desire, even here and now, to be the kind of people who can live in the paradise of God? To be blunt, do we prefer the eternal pleasures of God, or the fleeting pleasures of our sin?

Of course, we must be clear: God has not set up for us a lad-der of virtue which we must climb in order to ascend out of the mire of the human condition and into the heights of heaven. Even if such a ladder existed, we would not have the strength to climb it. God has descended to us and promised to pull all of heaven down after him, that it might fill every last nook and cranny of this universe. If we are believers in the gospel and therefore members of God's kingdom, then we will one day live in paradise, and we will be the kind of people who can live there. That is the promise of God; a promise backed up by the passion of his Son and the power of his Spirit.

The question is this: are we joyfully embracing this promise in our life right now? Are we already learning to savor the taste of God's great banquet, or are we still putting up with junk food? Are we beginning to adjust our eyes to the great daylight of God's glory by fixing them on Christ, or are we satisfied with the comforts of the world's dark night? Are we—to borrow a line from the great hymn—letting our hearts be tuned to sing God's grace?

Of course, heavenly mindedness is also very practical. Perhaps whoever said that heavenly mindedness detracts from the earthly good never tried very well at either. Heavenly-minded people are exactly what this lost and confused world needs, and goodness manifested in the world is what heaven desires. God's desire for his people, corporately and as individuals, is that they will learn to live out in the midst of this world, in some small measure, the value system of heaven. That is to say, our communities and our very bodies are locations at which Jesus's prayer that "Your will be done, your kingdom come on earth as it is in heaven" is to be fulfilled. And if this is to be fulfilled in our communities and in the activities of our bodies, it must also be fulfilled in our minds and in our hearts.

That is why Paul gives his audience a list of excellent things on which to dwell: *"Whatever is true, whatever is noble, whatever is right, whatever is pure, whatever is lovely, whatever is admirable—if anything is excellent or praiseworthy, set your minds on such things!"* Perhaps we can regard this list as a menu (at least the *hors devours* menu) of the delights of heaven.

Our world is broken, yet by grace it contains great beauties. We do not set our minds on the good, the true, and the beautiful because they are pleasant distractions from the world's strife, but because they are intrinsically worthy, and because they are what the world needs. We do not turn our gaze on these things so as to turn away from the world. We do not enjoy these blessed graces of God as if we were stealing ourselves away to a secret garden of private delights. No, we come to the garden to eat and drink so that we are refreshed and strengthened to turn back to the world, and from this garden we fill baskets of fruit to give generously to all in need. Perhaps this is a helpful test of whether or not something is good in our life: does it help us offer anything to the world around us? Does it help shape us into the kind of people who can share God's blessings with others? Contemplation of God does not ultimately mean turning away from the world, but turning toward it with a face that has beheld God's glory, and with lips that have spoken his praise.

It is easy to imagine the practices of contemplation, heavenly-mindedness, and soul-formation as excuses not to be about the hard work which needs doing in the world. Indeed, this is a perilous danger. The comfortable person who looks out upon a world filled with sufferings and crimes and injustices may sate himself with nice theological comforts: "What this world needs is simply for all these lost souls to draw close to God, so excuse me while I go attend to him myself." The person who says this may very nearly be right. He would be rightly shunning the error of the activist who seeks to make the world right without ever taking responsibility for that little corner of the world for which he is most chiefly responsible: his own heart. But the mistake here is to imagine that we can draw close to God without going to those places where he most desires to be present: among the lost, the sick, the poor, and the alone. Christ did not come to earth so he could sit quietly next to the pious in their rooms and smile approvingly at their prayers. He came to seek and save the lost; to get down with, in, and under the suffering and death of the world and to raise it up upon his broken and bleeding shoulders. When God came to the world, that is where he went, and he is still to be found there now. So when we consider how in our contemplation we can draw close to God, one of two things is true: either we will find him in the midst of the world's pain in the first place, or after God has met us in the quiet of our prayers, he will call us to follow him out into the turmoil of the world, where we shall become participants in our prayer's answers.

What it comes down to is this: contemplation and practice belong together, and in fact cannot be separated. To remove one from the equation is to nullify the other. We cannot rightly practice the work to which God has called us without nourishing our hearts on his goodness. And even if we could, we would be in the absurd position of bypassing the first and greatest commandment to get to the second. And yet, one cannot conceivably fulfill the first commandment to love God and set our hearts fully upon him without thereby being drawn into the enactment of his love for our neighbors.

Can we then read Paul's instruction this way? *Practice the truth. Practice nobility. Practice righteousness. Practice purity. Practice loveliness. Practice admirability, excellence, and praiseworthiness.* I think we must read the verse this way. But here we only see the clearer why we must first set our minds and hearts on these things. We cannot practice them as we should unless our minds have been saturated with them, dripping out in our every action.

So how are we to go about this? Let me list a few ideas simply as a starting place for the task of imagining what it might mean in our lives to "set your mind on such things." The following list does not represent any kind of studied expertise in mental well-being, but is simply a bit of common-sense. The reader is encouraged to add to the list. (Although again, it is helpful to ask these questions as we consider various practices: does this help me love God, and does this help me love others?)

- Read good books.
- Listen to good music.
- Spend time surrounded by beauty, especially in nature.
- Get physical exercise.
- Do good to others through simple acts of friendship, help, and kindness.
- Spend quality time with people who care about you and who are a positive influence on you—people you want to be like.
- Spend time also with a wider variety of people; especially people who can give you a fresh perspective on things. Have conversations in which you deeply and respectfully listen to others rather than focus on trying merely to get your own views across.

- Spend quality time with your family and friends. Have meals together, talk together, play games together.

- Take time practicing your own skills, hobbies, or other activities you enjoy. Make things, write things, play music, create art, play sports, cook meals, spend time in your shop—any activity which requires the productive use of the mind.

- Be careful in your consumption of news and social media. These can play an important role in maintaining connection to the world around us. But when they become habits or major time expenditures, they can have a very negative impact on our thought life.

- Get enough sleep.

- And of course, keep space in your life for the basic spiritual disciplines, especially Bible reading and prayer.

Speaking of prayer, it is not accidental that Paul in this passage progresses from a statement of God's nearness, to calling his audience not to be anxious, to instructing them to pray. All of our rejoicing and all our practices of attending to God-given goodness have their basis in the simple fact of God's presence. If we really know that God is near, and know this not just intellectually but with the life-shaping knowledge which is called faith, then joy will be available to us at all times. Even in the midst of fearful situations, we will not be overcome by anxiety. This is not to say that we will never feel fear or anxiety as emotions or states of mind. People are sometimes confused on this point, thinking that Christians must never experience fear, worry, or anxiety. Not to experience these emotions is not to be human. The belief that a good Christian will never feel afraid or anxious does not remove fear or anxiety, but merely piles guilt and shame on top of them. Scripture never commands us not to feel an emotion—indeed such a thing cannot be commanded—but simply to live in faith and obedience in light of the gracious presence of God, whatever our emotions might be. The person who knows the nearness of God is not someone who escapes all feelings of fear and anxiety, but someone who brings their fear and anxiety, with their whole self, into his presence. Fear and anxiety are therefore not altogether cancelled, but are rather robbed of their power to define our life or determine our actions. Our lives are then surrounded, even soaked, by the presence of God. In this world we will still have troubles and all their accompanying emotions. But neither those troubles nor those emotions have power to destroy us or blow us off the course which God has charted for our lives, for he has overcome the world. The peace of God which is beyond all understanding is not the total absence of fear, but rather the presence of God even in the face of our fears. The peace which comes from our knowledge of his presence will guard our hearts and minds from all the ravages which our fears threaten, even if we still feel these fears emotionally.

The faithful presence of God, which empties all the world's threats of their power, is also the reason why we pray. To pray is not to lob words up toward a distant being in the hopes that he might be listening. We pray because we know that God is already present. We believe that God is poised to answer our prayers because prayer itself is an answer to someone who has already come to us and addressed us. Too often we think of prayer as initiating a conversation with God in which we hope that he will respond. But God has already initiated the conversation with us by giving us his word, his Son, and his Spirit. His loving overture to us makes certain that our reply to him will be heard—indeed, that our words will go to his very heart. We have the confidence to go to God with our needs and requests because he has already come to us.

Prayer may be defined this way: it is deliberate personal attention to the personal presence of God. This is why prayer is about much more than just our words. It concerns the occupation of our minds and the attention of our hearts. Prayer is conversation with God, but more than that, it is rooted in a fundamentally conversational posture before him. We pray to God because of our needs and other things we want to express to him, but even more than that because of the relationship between us and God which he has already established. This relationship constantly forms us into the people he desires us to become. Prayer, therefore, is not only a proper expression of heavenly mindedness. It is a means by which heavenly mindedness grows in us, and by which we are shaped toward the likeness of Christ. After all, one of the best ways to share someone's mind and to become more like them is to spend time in quality conversation with them.

ON EARTH, OR IN HEAVEN?

Perhaps in all this we observe a deep tension between, on the one hand, having our mind in heaven, and on the other, focusing our minds on good earthly things. Perhaps this is a tension whose energy animates rather than impedes the Christian life. As was said before, it requires a heavenly mind to be of earthly good, and it requires a mind set on earthly goods to be of value to heaven's purposes.

Yet, perhaps a little more theological reflection shows this not to be quite as deep a paradox as first we thought. When we first hear the phrase "heavenly minded," it is all too easy for us to imagine a kind of surreal dreamscape of sky and clouds and harps. If we are tuned in to what the Bible says about heaven though, we are not thinking so much of an immaterial, ethereal afterlife where disembodied spirits dwell. Our thoughts are rather aimed toward the promise of bodily resurrection in the new heavens and the new earth—the place where God himself will make his dwelling among us. God has indeed crucified us with Christ to the old creation, but he has raised us into the new creation—a reality just as bodily and physical as the man who walked out of the grave on his own two feet, showed his wounds to his friends, and dined with them on broiled fish. The gospel of Jesus Christ is at once the denial of the world and the affirmation of all that is good in it. Again, that is no contradiction, for the problem with the world is not that it is a world of earth and water, and the problem with its people is not that they are people of flesh and blood, but that this world and its people have turned away from their creator. The goal of the new creation—what we often call heaven—is not that all flesh will be destroyed, but that "all flesh will see him together" (Isa 40:5). The days of groaning will be over, and the whole creation, led by the sons and daughters of God, will take up shouts of joyful praise. That day will not be the end of all songs; every song will then be a hymn of God's glory. That day will not be the end of all work; all work will then be worship. That day will not be the end of all human words; all words—even those spoken to one another—will be prayers to the most-high God. That day will not be the end of all art; all art will then shine with the beauty of the Lord. That day will not be the end of all human relationships and love; all true love will then be unmistakably seen as what it already is: the life of God lived in the fellowship of his creatures.

To be heavenly-minded, in the truest sense, is therefore to be attentive to all that is truly good even now, for all that is truly good on earth is already a little piece of heaven awaiting its full arrival. All good things have been created by God as reminders of his own goodness. Even the sand on the seashore and the stars in the sky are a billion shining fragments of his glory.

Of course, there is a stern warning attached to all this. It is all too possible to occupy ourselves with good things on earth and yet forget about God. In fact, that is largely the extent of what we sinful people do. All idols, and perhaps even all sins, are attempts to enjoy good things without enjoying God himself. Remember what we have already said: there are, in fact, no fundamentally evil desires, for nothing which is desirable is fundamentally evil. There are only evil strategies for fulfilling those desires; strategies which attempt to avoid God himself and his good purposes for us. But none of our "heavenly-mindedness," nor our earthly goods, have any value apart from the God by whom they were created, to whom they still point, and by whom they will all be perfected. Nothing is good which will not be used as an instrument of God's worship; and a good thing which itself is worshiped ceases to be good. There is nothing so tarnished that it cannot be redeemed to mirror God's glory, and there is nothing so pure that it cannot be made an idol. Perhaps more to the point, there is no person so righteous that he cannot be a rebel, and no soul so lost that he cannot be redeemed. Let us beware lest any good thing become a furnishing in the temple of our idols. As soon as we mistake a God-glorifying thing for God himself, it ceases to glorify him. Let no one confuse the creator and his creation. Nature can only speak God's words in an echo; those who turn merely to her to see their God find only idols and despair.

The key to all of this, then, is to attend to the excellent things God has given us with God himself at the center. Anything that is truly good, whether found on earth or in heaven, has the source of its goodness in God himself. When Paul directs us to turn our minds toward excellent and praiseworthy things, he is ultimately directing our attention toward God himself. Consider again Paul's words: "*Whatever is true, whatever is noble, whatever is right, whatever is pure, whatever is lovely, whatever is admirable—if anything is excellent or praiseworthy—set your minds on such things.*" What is more true than the author of all truth? What is more noble than the majesty of God? What is more right than his righteousness? What is more pure than his perfection? Is there anything lovelier than his love? Is there anything more deserving of our admiration? What in heaven or earth surpasses God in excellence? Who is there, in this world or any other, so deserving of our praise?

If we follow Paul's instructions here, we will surely turn our minds toward many good things with which God has filled our lives, and to do this is most profitable. But if we follow these instructions to the utmost; to their very end, our attention will be focused on God. Indeed, all the excellent things of heaven and earth matter for nothing unless they are means by which we engage in the most intrinsically worthwhile activity of all: the enjoyment of God himself.

That is why the highest command is to rejoice. We sometimes think that commandments are odious, burdensome things; instructions which are grudgingly obeyed only to avert something even more unpleasant. But how wrong we are: beneath all the commandments of Scripture; beneath all the laws of Israel; beneath even the great commandments to love God and neighbor; is the greatest commandment of all: rejoice! For to rejoice, in the truest sense of the word, is simply to delight in the one source of joy, which is God himself. The greatest commandment was said by Jesus to be the love of God. What is it to love God but to enjoy him supremely; to be completely satisfied in his sufficiency; to be utterly happy in his happiness? And what is it to love one's neighbor, but to tell him or her, "Here are the riches of God's table; let us sit down and feast together!"

Indeed, God's great desire is for his creatures to be happy. But there is a common confusion on this point. We think that it means God writes us a free pass to do whatever we think will bring us happiness. That is a doctrine which will, ironically, only make us unhappy. God wants us to be happy in the only true happiness there is, which is God himself. As the Psalmist put it, "Delight yourself in the LORD, and he will give you the desires of your heart." Or we could paraphrase it this way: "Make God himself the object of your desire and delight, and God will see that desire fulfilled." In a God-centered universe, being truly happy does not mean doing whatever we want; it means wanting what God desires for us. And his desire is that we will know him and be known by him; that we will love him as we enjoy his love, and make his love known to all the world.

That is why we are to occupy our minds with good things. God in his grace has filled this world with countless little things designed to remind us of him; a thousand compass needles drawn by the magnet of his glory; a million mirrors in which to look and see that the Lord is God. But above all, however else we fix our minds on that which is excellent, we must draw our great delight from God himself.

Once again, the contemplation of God's goodness is not only our deep pleasure but the world's great need. This entire broken creation awaits the promise of her creator and the fulfillment of Jesus's prayer: "On earth as it is in heaven." If we in our minds and hearts are already directing our attention, our desire, and our delight on the good things of God which he has created and has promised to recreate, and if above all our delight is in the goodness and glory of God himself, then already a bit of heaven is here on earth. That is the healing which this world needs. That is the river which will begin to water its droughted fields.

And not just that: it is the reason you and I and all things have been created: for God's glorious desire and mankind's great delight.

CONCLUSION

Morty was a man of simple tastes. His dinner was the same every day—a cheeseburger and fries from the nearby drivethrough restaurant. One day, as he was sitting in his apartment watching TV, a mysterious figure appeared standing in front of him, clothed in white and shining like the noonday sun. Morty was terrified, but the man said, "Morty, do not be afraid. I am an angel of the Lord, and today you must come with me to heaven. Tonight you are to be the guest of honor at the Lord's banquet table."

In a moment, Morty found himself seated in the presence of the Lord at a great table which groaned under the weight of a luxurious feast. Here were gourmet foods from all around the world—more dishes than Morty even knew existed. The Lord held out his hand and said, with a voice that boomed with a kind of jolly thunder, "Morty, you are the guest of honor tonight at my table. Dine with me and eat from my table all that your heart desires!"

Morty looked up and down the long table, but all the food appeared strange to him. "Please, good sir," he asked the Lord, "might I have a cheeseburger and fries?"

"I have better food than that, my son," said the Lord. "Tonight is a special occasion. There are many years yet before it is your time to join me again in my presence. You will have time to eat many cheeseburgers if you like until then. But now you may feast on all your heart can desire and more. It's my treat!"

But Morty said, "Oh Lord, I have never eaten anything so strange and foreign as what I see here. Please just let me go back and get my cheeseburger from the drive-through."

Oh, the feast of the Lord's table is rich! But it is an acquired taste. May he grant it to us to desire all that is truly good.

But Our Citizenship Is in Heaven

In the gleam of morning light
In the starlit paths of night
In the splendor of the skies
Beauty bathes our careworn eyes,
And You are there—our heart's delight.

On the mountain cloaked in snow
In the florid field below
In the forest, dark and green
Silence speaks of things unseen,
And You are there—and our hearts know.

In the flashing of the fire
In the pine tree's lonely choir
In the surging of the sea
Longing lures us out to Thee,
And You are there—our heart's desire.

8

The Riches of His Glory
The Christ-Shaped Life as Gratitude and Generosity

PHILIPPIANS 4:10-23

I was delighted in the Lord to discover your renewed thought-fulness toward me. Indeed, you had no opportunity in the past to express your thoughtfulness to me. I do not say this out of personal need, for I have learned to be content in all situations. I know what it's like to live in the humblest circumstances, and what it's like to live with an abundance. In every and all situations, I have learned the secret of contentment: to have my stomach well-filled, or having to go hungry; to have an abundance or to go without. I am able to do it all through the one who strengthens me. Yet it was good of you to share in my sufferings!

And you know, Philippians, that when you were first beginning in the gospel, when I left Macedonia, no church shared with me in the way of giving or receiving, except you alone. Even when I was in Thessalonica, you sent me help for my needs more than once. It's not that I'm pursuing you for another gift; I am rather pursuing the increase of credit given to you. I have received all I need and more. I've received the full gift from you through Epaphroditus. It is like a fragrant incense; a sacrifice acceptable and pleasing to God. And my God will fill your every need according to the riches of his glory in Christ Jesus. Glory be to God our Father in this age and the age to come, Amen!

Greet all of God's holy people in Christ Jesus, as your brothers and sisters who are with me send their greetings to you. All God's holy people greet you, especially those from the house of Caesar. The grace of the Lord Jesus Christ be with your spirit.

How do we grow into the Christ-shaped life? That is the question we have been pursuing from the beginning of this book, and by now it should be clear that the answer involves participation in the Christ-shaped community. To be drawn into the Christ-shaped life is to be drawn into the fellowship of like-minded humility, servitude, and love. This is a fellowship marked both by gospel-suffering and gospel-joy. The cross has created a community of self-giving love, a community created in the image of the self-giving Christ—indeed, in the image of the self-giving relations of the eternal Trinity.

In this closing passage of Philippians, we see as clear a portrait as ever what this community looks like in action. Here Paul is not spelling out abstract theology, but is rather speaking in directly interpersonal terms with a community of people whom he loves and who love him in return. He speaks about the very practical matter of giving and receiving gifts for his ministry; about why he is not asking them for more and why he is satisfied and content with his present situation, yet also about why he is so thankful for their past generosity.

But these practical interpersonal matters have a profoundly deep theological foundation, as Paul clearly indicates. He explains how the Philippians' gifts to him have been a means by which they have shared in his ministry of cruciform suffering for the sake of the gospel. There was a point at which they alone showed a unique concern for Paul expressed through material giving. Paul clearly sees this as much more than a practical aid. In fact, he almost bends over backwards to stress how much he is not dependent on their gifts, since his needs have been well met by God's provision, and he has learned profound lessons of material contentment. But their gift is important in this way: it is the expression of a deep mutual fellowship in the gospel, in which, by sacrificially giving their resources, they have joined in Paul's sacrificial giving of his life for the gospel, and by extension, in Christ's ultimate sacrifice, of which Paul is an apostolic servant. Such giving is, to use terms drawn from the Old Testament law, a fragrant and pleasing offering to God. It is an acceptable act of worship, and Paul assures them that what they have given in material resources will be well compensated by what they will receive from God: not only God's loving, providential care for their own material needs, but also that which is immeasurably greater: enjoyment of the riches of God's glory, which is already theirs in Christ.

The theological upshot of this passage, therefore, is this: to share with one another by giving and receiving, as well as to share in each other's sufferings, is to participate in the Trinitarian economy of grace and glory. We partake in "the riches of his glory in Jesus Christ" by giving freely and joyfully to one another. This kind of reciprocity of giving is what has always built and nourished the bonds of human community and fellowship. This is a deep truth of God's kingdom. At the same time, however, this is in fact an area in which we most clearly see the image of God in almost all human communities. Humans, according to their fallen nature, have lost touch with God himself, but they have not entirely lost touch with the fundamental, even trinitarian truth that life, love, and meaning are found (or can at least be glimpsed) in the sharing of good things.

This passage points us directly toward such foundational truths. The very meaning of being human before God, of existing in conformity with his eternal purposes, is to be a participant in the economy of divine love and glory. God purposed humans from the beginning to be creatures who receive good things from him and then partake in the manifold joy of sharing those good things with one another, being both beloved recipients of God's goodness and agents for sharing God's goodness with all of creation. This fundamental human purpose receives a unique fulfillment in God's holy people, the church. We are a fellowship of people who have received the unfathomable riches of God in Christ and continue to receive every good thing from the Spirit, and who joyfully share these gifts with one another and with the world around us. By doing so, we express love and worship and glory back to God.

To grow into the Christ-shaped life, then, means not only growing in likeness to Christ, but also attaining through the grace of the Holy Spirit such glorious union with him that we stand with him in the trinitarian communion of self-giving love. In other words, we stand with the Son in receiving love from the Father and in giving glory back to him, all through the Holy Spirit.

Again, we are most poignantly reminded that the Christ-shaped life is not a solitary thing, but one embodied by our life together as God's people. It is a life of joyfully sharing good things from God and giving the glory back to him. It is a life lived by freely and joyfully giving, and discovering in this process not sorrowful poverty but the blessed abundance which is Christlike contentment in the riches of God's glory.

To unpack the lesson for us in more detail, we might talk about two deeply related disciplines: the discipline of gospel gratitude/contentment, and the discipline of gospel giving.

GOSPEL GRATITUDE/CONTENTMENT

Paul says, "*I have learned to be content in all situations. I know what it's like to live in the humblest circumstances, and what it's like to live with an abundance. In every and all situations, I have learned the secret of contentment: to have my stomach well-filled, or having to go hungry; to have an abundance or to go without. I am able to do it all through the one who strengthens me.*" This is Paul's explanation for why he is not begging the Philippians for more gifts. He wants to express deep gratitude for their financial partnership with him, but he is very careful that in doing so he does not imply that he is demanding more from them. To this end, Paul makes a moving statement about contentment in all situations. He has learned how to get by with either much or with very little.

Perhaps this sounds at first like a boast of stoicism, as if Paul's contentment were grounded in his own moral toughness. If this were the case, Paul's contentment would have its source in his own inner resources. As it is, though, his contentment is nourished by the riches of Christ's power, which transforms even poverty into abundance.

Perhaps this is a needed corrective to some of our assumptions about contentment. It is natural to think of contentment as a kind of stoicism. Whereas some might boast of their great wealth, others might make a boast of their ability to live happily with little. The substance of that boast might lie in the claim that they have overcome all greed or materialistic desires, or perhaps in their great resourcefulness and cleverness whereby they live self-sufficiently. But Christian contentment is neither a moralism nor a self-sufficiency. It is rather a lived celebration of the all-sufficient goodness of Christ which God freely gives us. Our contentment should not have its basis in any special ability of our own, but rather in the great ability and generosity of God, whereby he has promised to meet our every need. In other words, the Christian discipline of contentment is inseparable from the Christian discipline of gratitude. We are content because we are glad and grateful recipients of God's gifts to us in Christ.

To be content is therefore an expression of our deepest and highest calling to rejoice in the goodness of God himself. If we have everything in the world except God himself, we have nothing, and our hearts will ache with ceaseless hunger. But if we have nothing in the world except God himself, we have everything, and our hearts will rejoice in the fulness of all that is good. For there is nothing worth having which is not found in God himself. This is the logic of the Christ-shaped life—which is no surprise, since it is the logic of the kingdom of God which Christ himself so eloquently taught (see especially Matt 6:19–34).

If we really know God and are bound to him through Christ and the Spirit, the evidence will surface eventually in the form of a strong desire for his presence and deep contentment with his goodness. For what is there we could rightly desire other than God himself, and all the goodness of his being which is his pleasure to share with us?

If we think about this truth carefully, though, we will understand that mature Christian contentment with God is not a monkish indifference to all our physical needs. The point is not that these do not matter; the point is knowing that they matter to God. It isn't that food and clothing and health are unimportant. It is rather the case that, precisely because they are good and important parts of God's creative plan for us, they can be known to have their source in the God who delights to give us everything we need. If God is good, then all truly good things must somehow matter in his sight even more than in ours. And even if we die in poverty and suffering (as indeed many saints have), we can die knowing that we are destined for a resurrection in which we will know a life of joyful physical abundance from God which now can scarcely be imagined.

Perhaps the matter is best summed up in the simple truth that in Christ, God has given us his ultimate gift: the gift of his very life; indeed, his very self. To be a recipient of the gift of Christ through the gospel is the fundamental meaning of our Christian identity and existence. Therefore, the disciplines of gratitude and contentment must lie at the center of our Christian life. The Christ-shaped life is a life not only shaped by imitating him, but also by receiving him as God's supreme gift, and therefore receiving a life shaped into the posture of gratitude and contentment. To have Christ, and to know that he has us, is to be joyously thankful and supremely happy. (Little wonder that Philippians is known as the epistle of joy!)

GOSPEL GIVING

In this passage, we see various dimensions of the relationship between gratitude, contentment, and giving. Paul expresses great thankfulness for the Philippians' gifts, but he also expresses his contentment, so that they will know that he is not asking for more. Paul's contentment, in turn, is grounded in the riches of the gifts he has already received from God; gifts assured by the ultimate gift of the gospel of Jesus Christ. Based on the logical flow implied in all of this (God gives gifts to his people, they share these gifts with one another, they are satisfied, and God is glorified),[1] Paul assures his audience that God will indeed "fill your every need from the riches of his glory." In other words, Paul is telling them that even though they have poured themselves out, they will not run dry, for God will richly fill and refill their every need. This kind of assurance will encourage their future generosity to one another and to the rest of God's church. People sometimes are reluctant to give because they fear that they will run out of what they need to care for themselves, but those who are assured of God's provision are set free to share generously with all in need. Because God gives, we can share with others. In fact, the mutual generosity of God's people is often the means by which God provides for our needs.

At this point, however, a clarification is in order. We must insist on a distinction between the teaching of this passage and that of the prosperity gospel, which typically trades in manipulative and false promises: "Give to my ministry and God will bless you!" The message of the gospel is almost the reverse of this. God has already

1. Briones, "Why Can't We Be Friends?," 45.

blessed us. Therefore we give in such a way as to honor him and one another. We give in proportion to that which we have received. Have you received much in the way of financial or other material goods? Then give of them generously. Are you poor in money but rich in time? Then give of your time. Give in all the areas that God has given to you. Give your abilities. Give your words—of advice, and better yet, of encouragement. Give your perspective: God has created no other pair of eyes exactly like yours to see the world. Above all, give richly in grace, mercy, and forgiveness, for these God has poured out to us most lavishly.

Once again, this logic is deeply rooted in the gospel itself. Recall what has been said many times now about the shape of Christ's life and ministry (most directly described in Phil 2:6–11): Jesus, though endowed from all eternity with the riches of divinity, laid down his claim to those heavenly riches when he came to earth as a humble servant. He freely poured out the riches of his righteousness and love for a poor and starving world. Therefore, God lifted him up, honoring him forever in the splendor of heaven's glory and by the praise of all creatures.

That is the means by which God has given to us—and not merely given the physical blessings of this present life. This is how God has gifted us with eternity. As God's people, we are called to embrace and participate in this same life-shape as was embodied and enacted by Christ. We too, having been richly graced by God, are to pour ourselves out for one another and for the needs of the world around us. We do so empowered by the inexhaustible riches of God's gift already given in Christ, and assured by the promise that as we give, God (who has given us his very self) will also supply us with all we need for daily life.

The Christ-shaped life, then, is not merely an inward piety. It is as practical and tangible as our budget and our bank account—not to mention all the other ways we can give to one another through our physical resources and activities. Whether in their time, talent, or treasure, the people being remade in the image of their Savior are to be people who continually give of themselves to others for Christ's sake, empowered by his generosity past and assured by his generosity future. It is no accident that so much of Jesus's preaching and teaching featured calls to live generously as we trust God to meet our needs. The kingdom of God has an economy, though not one driven by markets and consumers and interest rates. The economy of the kingdom is driven by generosity and the kind of self-giving love that flows from the trinitarian God. The Christ-shaped life is one which partakes in this kingdom economy taught and exemplified by Jesus himself.

There is yet another practical (and deeply theological) aspect of gospel-giving. As mentioned above, the giving and receiving of gifts has always been at the heart of human relationships and community. In nearly all human cultures, gift-giving functions in some way or another as a means for creating, maintaining, or celebrating relational bonds between persons or communities. Again, that may be regarded as a way in which human nature, even in its fallen state, still reflects the image of God. God himself has always been a giver. To exist as a creature is to be a recipient of God's gift of creation. *Gift* therefore lies irremovably at the heart of our relationship with God; a relationship which grounds our very existence. The God-world relationship cannot be anything other than a giver-receiver relationship. It is at least a dim reflection of this fact that all human relationships involve some form of a gift dynamic. For example, any human friendship worthy of being so designated is not something that can be earned. We may earn a person's services, admiration, or even their trust. But love, by its very essence, is something never earned, only freely given.

While all human persons and communities participate in this truth, those who receive the gifts of God in Christ do so most fully. The community of God, his church, consists of those who have been drawn back into the Creator-creature relationship as it was meant to be from the beginning. God's gift of love and life, given most perfectly in Christ Jesus, has created a community of fellowship; a society of brothers and sisters bound in love to God through Christ and the Holy Spirit, and therefore also to one another.

This is the relational situation in which Christian generosity lives. We give, as the Philippian believers did, as an expression of the fellowship which exists between us as members of Jesus Christ and as participants in his life, sufferings, death, and resurrection.

We are therefore called as Christians to embrace an existential posture of generosity. We as humans were created to be outward-facing creatures. We were meant to live with our faces turned upward and our hands held outward. Christians are those who, by being drawn into the life of Jesus Christ and shaped into his likeness, return to such a posture. This means that generosity ought to permeate our lives in every way. Not only are we to give generously of our money and other physical resources. The whole of our life is to be regarded as a gift: a gift received from God and now passed on joyfully to others.

Therefore, we are not to be in the habit of clinging to our things, our time, or our lives, as if they were our own. Those who so cling to their lives will lose them, for life cannot long endure in the iron grip of selfish individualism. All real life is a gift and a giving. Even as we constantly fall short, we must never cease to long for the kind of life which is our promised inheritance, in which our hearts and our hands are constantly open to those around us. We can make it our work in the here and now to begin embracing this life as the Spirit of God enables us to do so. The human heart was not meant to be a fortress of safety and solitude. It was meant to be a fountain supplied by the living water of God, constantly filled by him and constantly overflowing to those around us. We have a long way to go before the waters flow freely. But God has promised that they will, and happy are those who begin to live that way today.

Can our churches learn to function this way, as fellowships of self-giving love, drawing on the abundance of God and joyfully sharing it together? That is the reality in which, by which, and for which the church was created. We are created to need God and also to need one another. The church is meant to inhabit this truth of creation, and to exemplify it before the watching world. The modern ideal of individual self-sufficiency is foreign to the life of God's people, which is a fellowship of mutual service and generosity. We are all to be constantly reminded that we as individuals are not sufficient, whether for our material needs or for our happiness. We are meant to be a people who, by our mutual support and fellowship, draw together on the abundant sufficiency of God.

CONCLUSION

As we have seen, the book of Philippians is all about a journey: the pilgrimage toward our true home. This home, however, is not so much a place in which we arrive, but a place which arrives in us. The pilgrimage is the process by which the kingdom grows within our hearts. Through Christ it has already staked its claim in us. A day is coming when the seed will come to full flower and bear its fruit, and every inch of our being—and indeed, every inch of this universe—will shine with the radiance of God's glory: the glory of the trinitarian, Christ-shaped life. This is a life which has already been given to us, is already ours, yet remains a promise for the future awaiting its full completion. The Christian life, then, is the pilgrimage in which we progress toward our God-given destiny of conformity to the image and likeness of Jesus Christ. The journey is marked by the growth of rightly attuned desires and self-giving service for the sake of the gospel.

As we see at the end of Philippians, contentment and generosity play an important role in our journey. Our growth toward right desires is always a growth toward God as the supreme source and goal of all our desires—the true object of our heart's contentment. Such satisfaction in God empowers us to live generously—and of course, generosity is one of the most important practical manifestations of self-giving love after the pattern of Christ. The generosity of God's people is an enacted parable of the gospel, and an imitation of their savior. "For you know the grace of our Lord Jesus Christ, that though he was rich, yet for your sake he became poor, so that you through his poverty might become rich" (2 Cor 8:9).

And of course, we are also reminded that Christian fellowship is essential to our journey. We have been forged by the gospel, and for the gospel's sake, into a fellowship of mutual love and service.

None of our lives is ours alone, for we all belong to the Lord, and therefore to one another.

On one level, this is as practical as anybody's travel plans ever were. Well-known is the saying: "If you want to travel fast, go alone. If you want to travel far, go together." The only way we will arrive at our goal is if we press on to take hold of that for which Christ took hold of us—and take hold of it together, helping one another along through mutual encouragement, edification, and service.

But togetherness is not only practical travel advice. It is itself the goal. Our very identity has been forged through our union with the crucified and risen Christ, and therefore with all who likewise share union with him. Fellowship is essential to what we are as Christians. Our final destiny is a fully-formed fellowship of love. Gathered around God's throne, shining like stars in reflection of his glory, we will forever sing his song, our many voices gathered up into that mighty chord of triune love.

O Lord, how I have longed to lift my voice and sing!
But there are no songs on earth great enough to tell your glory,
And if there were, my lips would be too weak to sing them.
Alas, I cannot find my tune;
The songless world shudders in the night.

But there is a song already sung,
A song to rouse the world from sleepless slumbers,
A song to wake the dead, to end the night.
Your song was sounded in the darkest hour
From lips too parched to sip a sodden sponge.
The God-forsaken voice of God has spoken,
Word before all worlds has sung!

How mighty is your song, O Lord,
Your servant-song of triune Love!
Your trumpet echoes in the highest heaven,
Your bells reverberate in soundless depths.
Your voice resounds in all creation,
Let all other voices join and sing:
Reed and willow, bubbling brook,
Crackling fire, surging sea, and birds
On every branch do not withhold your praise.

So teach, O Lord, my faltering lips your song.
Purge them with holy fire from your altar drawn.
Give me a better word than my own tongue can forge,
O Word of Love before all worlds began.
Let your mighty chord, the song of triune love,
My anthem ever be.
O Lord, how I have longed to lift my voice and sing!

Conclusion

THE GOSPEL OF PHILIPPIANS

THE MESSAGE OF PHILIPPIANS, and indeed the message of the whole New Testament, has at its heart the truth that Christian faith is not a means to an end, but is an end in itself. In Philippians, the gospel of Jesus Christ is described not as a legal loophole for escaping eternal punishment or squeaking through heaven's door, but as a shape and pattern of life which is intrinsically excellent. To be a Christian is not simply to have made a decision for Christ at some point in our lives. It is for one's entire life to be conformed to the pattern of his death and resurrection. This is not, in the final analysis, a sacrifice which is made worthwhile by a good final return on our investment. To be a follower of Christ—or we could also say, to be a participant in Christ—is itself the ultimate and perhaps the only worthwhile thing there is: to be drawn into the divine communion of self-giving love.[1]

Too many Christians, I believe, have an impoverished view of the gospel. Too many only know what Dallas Willard called a "gospel of sin management."[2] This is a view of the gospel that only

---

1. Roger Olson put this well: "[A]uthentic Christianity is not about giving up sinful pleasures to avoid hell. And it is not about witnessing to others about Jesus the Savior to keep them out of hell. What, then, is it about? Authentic Christianity is about being in communion with God through Jesus Christ the Savior and receiving the Holy Spirit to give life-fulfilling love, joy, and peace." Olson, "Test of the Authenticity of Your Christianity."

2. Willard, *Divine Conspiracy*, 35–59.

goes as far as a message about escaping the judgement of God. Of course, this is indeed a vital part of the gospel. But it is not complete unless we address the larger question: what exactly are we saved *from*, and even more importantly, what are we saved *for*, and saved *to*? If we are, as is sometimes implied, saved from the tyrannical demands of a merciless God (by the hand of a loving demigod named Jesus), not only have we abandoned the truth of the scriptures, but we no longer have a gospel. The good news is no longer good. For how can there be any truly good news in this universe if the God who runs it is not himself radiantly good?

The gospel, then, is not the story of a loving Jesus who saves us from a harsh and cruel God (again, that would not really be good news at all). The gospel is the good news that God himself has come to us in the person of the Son, Jesus Christ, and that in and through his self-giving love, he has saved us from ourselves—from the evil in which we are complicit; from our rebellion against his goodness. The gospel is the good news that the one who created this world is absolutely good and absolutely loving, and that his goodness and love have reached out to rescue us and the entire world from the evil which lives in it and in us.

But that is not all. The gospel is the good news that this amazing God, who has rescued us from our sin and the judgement it incurs, is gathering us once again to his side, to live once again as we were created to live, and to be once again that which we were created to be: a holy people made in the image of a holy God; a people of faith, hope, and love; a people gathered into the eternal joy of his glory. In short, a people formed by and after the pattern of Christ himself. The gospel is the good news that God, in his goodness, wisdom, and love, has not only saved us from judgement through Christ, but has welcomed us into the very life for which we were created: the Christ-shaped life of triune love.

Perhaps many Christians begin their new life in Christ primarily in fear of God's judgement. Perhaps that is not all bad. Sin is a serious matter—deadly serious. To fear the wrath of God is not a foolish thing. It is in fact the beginning of wisdom.

But it is not wisdom's end. If our gospel is no bigger than an escape from judgement, we will never grow to understand the beauty of our salvation, and indeed the beauty of God. We will never grow into the maturity of the Christ-shaped life until we learn to see the love and glory of God in Christ; until we learn to love him and trust him for who he is and not merely for a service he renders us. We will not understand the glory of the gospel until we see that it is not merely a means to an end, but an end in itself. The glory of the gospel is not that there is a loophole by which we can escape the judgement of God, but rather that the God who judges is infinitely worth knowing, loving, and worshiping, and that he himself in Christ and the Spirit redeems sinners like us back to his side. Merely fleeing from the punishment of God will not move us to worship him. But that is the goal of the gospel: not just that we will escape God's judgement, but that we will enjoy his love forever—and that we will in fact become the kind of persons who can enjoy it.

Christianity, then, is not a loophole. It is not a life raft. It is liberty. It is love. It is the longing of our hearts. It is the grand and joyful adventure of knowing God by participating in the Christ-shaped life.

LOSING OUR VOICE

There are other problems too with thinking of Christianity merely as a means to an end. Suppose that the gospel of Christ is just a loophole which can be jumped through at one point in life which then frees up the rest of our life for other concerns. In this case, Christ occupies a designated corner of our heart as "Savior," but the rest of our life becomes functionally our own. We've agreed to let Christ be our Suffering Servant to save us for eternity, but our life now is still all about pursuing the dreams of power and success which the world places before us.

So it is that much of modern Christianity has lost its voice. We were created and redeemed to join in singing God's song of triune love; the great melody which called the world into existence and will go on into all eternity. In our present lives, so early on our journey, we are only beginning to learn our pilgrim song. Even at the best of times, we sing in a faltering tone. But we as a church, if we are to exist as such at all, must have our ear tuned to the song of God—the great anthem sung out to the world by Christ in his death and resurrection. But sometimes it seems that we lose the tune entirely. The song of humble servant love (the very power and glory of God!) is drowned out by songs of human power and glory; songs of pride and pedigree; songs of might and money; songs of sex and success. There are throbbing anthems of bombastic nationalism. There are pulsing rhythms of wanton consumerism. And of course, there are countless little ditties which are all about "me." The world is shaken to pieces by the din. In the midst of the cacophony, we forget the voice of Jesus. And so it is that we too, his beloved church, begin to lose our voice.

Just how has the church lost her voice? We could point to many examples, both throughout history and also with an eye to the present day. We think about the tragedies of church history, when all too often the church became an agent of militaristic oppression rather than of servant love. The crusades and other bloody religious wars, the abusive and arrogant colonialism which was sometimes practiced against Native Americans and other indigenous peoples, and the support of slavery in America all come to mind. Here we see the long and dark legacy of a church that has often thought of itself as an imperial ruler of the world rather than the body of the suffering servant. Christianity today, even in the twilight of Christendom, is still hanging on to dreams of this kind of temporal dominion. But have God's people ever truly represented him well when they have attempted to do so from a position of dominance in the world? Has not the church always most clearly sung the song of her savior when she has known herself to be a pilgrim people, a voice crying in the wilderness, performing works of servant love and speaking words of prophetic truth from the margins rather than from the center of power? Surely raising such questions demands a much longer discussion, and we should resist the temptation to settle for easy cliches about the corrupting influences of power. Surely the history of Christianity is much more complex and multi-dimensional than this. Yet can we read a document like Paul's letter to the Philippians, which constantly repeats the anthem of humble service for the sake of Christ after his own cruciform pattern, and avoid the conclusion that throughout much of history, the church has lost its voice?

We could well examine the church in America today and come to a similar conclusion. Perhaps we think first of the many tragic failures of leadership in the church, in which all too many respected pastors and other leaders have been revealed to be deeply enmeshed in sinful lifestyles and the abuse of power. Perhaps the truth of the matter, though, is that these failures are but the symptom of a much deeper and more pervasive disease: a failure of discipleship in the church.

This is not a question of the church producing perfect people (we know better than to expect that), but too often, the entire value system of the church seems to be out of alignment with the value system of heaven as it is depicted in Philippians and the rest of the New Testament. It is not merely a lack of depth and attention in the church's discipleship—although that surely is a part of it. Too often, the church propagates what we could call a mis-discipleship of its members. Instead of being formed to resemble Jesus Christ, both individuals and whole churches end up looking nothing like him. Many churches are, in practice, designed to disciple their members to be comfortable consumers of a "worship experience," conformers to the social and moral norms of the modern Christian subculture, patriotic right-wing Americans, or trendy left-wing social justice warriors. Yet none of these things lie at the heart of what it means to be a disciple of Jesus Christ—a person formed after his own image. Is it any wonder that many Christians attend church for years, yet never confront their deep habitual sins such as pride, arrogance, bitterness, anger, jealousy, or lack of self-discipline? These kinds of malformations in Christian character sabotage our relationships, our leadership, and our very souls. Yet they often go ignored, so focused we become on those aspects of our image and lifestyle which lie closer to the surface.

How did we get here? How is it that the church, designed to be conformed to the image of the crucified Christ, has so often lost its voice? That is not a question which can really be addressed at the end of a book like this one; it is a question for the beginning of a different kind of book (and surely a much longer one.) But I would suggest, as I already have, that a big part of the problem lies in making Jesus Christ and his gospel a means to an end rather than an end in itself.

Part of this problem is the neglect of real discipleship in favor of a utilitarian approach to Christianity, which is all about the achievement of certain benchmarks of apparent success. This can appear in a number of guises, including "easy-believe" evangelism, a focus on people-pleasing, consumeristic trends, or (ironically) an emphasis on narrow legalisms and dogmatisms that define the "pure church" but neglect the substance of Christ and his gospel of grace. Or perhaps, we have been taught to equate the success of Christianity with winning certain culture-war battles rather than the presence of subversive worship and servant love. In all of the above trends, we see a kind of utilitarianism creep into our Christianity. These are views of Christian faith that are all about signing the dotted lines to get souls into heaven, perfecting the church according to a humanistic, legalistic vision, or a culture-war mentality which is more about winning public battles than maintaining a faithful witness to the sacrificial victory of the Lamb.

In perhaps all these ways, we begin to habitually think of God and his gospel as a means to an end rather than an end in itself. Much modern preaching and worship in the church is self-centered by nature. God and his word are treated as useful tools for having a better life now. The gospel is seen as a means to the end of having a better life for eternity. Christianity becomes a resource or a weapon for fighting culture war battles.

But God and his gospel should be most loved by us and attended to by us not because they are powerful instruments, but because they are true, and because they are utterly good and most inherently worthy of our love and attention. The life of the church must be directed in this direction: toward the inherent beauty, truth, and goodness of God and his gospel. This is where the real power of transformational discipleship lies—not when we seek it by means of God, but when we seek God first through Christ, and as a result of this, find ourselves on the path toward becoming more like him.

Let me offer an example which perhaps strikes closer to home than all these generalities. How often, when the Bible is preached, do we need either some kind of captivating introduction or a practical application to make us sit up and listen to what the text has to say? To be clear, I'm not even remotely suggesting that preachers should stop employing the devices of introduction and application in their sermons. The biblical texts themselves use similar means of communication, and the Bible's messages must indeed be applied to life. The problem I'm getting at lies closer to the heart: we are not inherently interested in God, in what he has done for us, and in what he has to say to us. We only become interested when we see God connected to something of more immediate proximity to my life. If someone who is important to us, whom we love, speaks to us, do we not want to listen? And how much more, if the holy creator of the universe has spoken to us, should we not be infinitely interested in what he has to say? If God addressing us, saving us, and drawing us to himself is not inherently interesting to us, then there is something wrong with us. That's putting it bluntly, but I think that this is precisely our problem, both as a church and as individuals within it. We are not inherently interested in God. We are not, to use Paul's language, "preoccupied with Christ." We only, at best, become interested when we realize that God and his gospel are somewhat useful for us. This proves that there is something deeply and terribly wrong with us.

I don't mean this in a critical or judgmental way. I must own this personally: there is something very much wrong with me. Here is where I, the author, must come closest to the heart of the matter. It is easy for me to critique the proud and bloody history of the church, or to lament fallen leaders of the church today, or to aim my barbs of prophetic rebuke at all the failures of discipleship which lie beneath these more obvious problems. But the real problem lies within me as much as it lies anywhere else, and it boils down to this: I do not love God even remotely as much as God deserves to be loved. I do not come close to wanting to be like Christ as much as God wants me to be like him. The truth is, I am more interested in myself than I am in God. This is the horrible, hellish secret of my heart. And I suspect that I am not alone.

LEARNING TO SING

But there is good news for the world, for the church, and even for me: God has loved us outrageously through his servant Jesus Christ. He has loved us so much that he has promised us that we who believe will be like him. He has already planted the seeds of the Christ-shaped life in our heart. He has claimed our souls for his kingdom. This is the promise of God, and his omnipotent mercy will see all of his promises fulfilled. The day is coming, sooner or later, when you, me, all the church, and the entire consummated creation will abound with the joy of God's self-giving love. The song still sounds strange to our ears. But it is already the song of our life, and one day we will sing it with all our heart.

This leaves us with a question. Are we learning to desire this promised future; to truly set our hearts upon it? Perhaps none of us, in the present order of things, desire God the way we should. But are we at least desiring to desire God? Are we learning to agree with God about our terrible problem, and about the solution to this problem, which is God himself given to us in Christ? Are we learning to rejoice in the destiny he has set before us of conformity to the gospel of self-giving love? Are we, God's people, learning to sing our hymn of amazing grace, to rejoice in what God has done for us, and in what, by his mercy, we shall become? The day may be far away when we can sing of our perfection, but we can already sing of the perfection of Christ. And as we sing, so shall we begin to glimmer with the light of his glory.

Now is a time when the voice of Jesus needs to be heard in all the world, now as much as it ever has. When will we, the people who bear the name of Christ, cease merely to echo the anthems of the world? God has given us a better song.

But it takes courage to lift our voice and sing. The song of the cross is a scandal to the world. The powers of this age tolerate no affront to their sacred alters of pride. The way of humility and love and peace is no mere nuisance to the world who crucified its savior. It is an outrage. So it is that we lose heart. Our lips falter and the song of Christ grows faint upon our lips.

But if we belong to him, sing we shall. It is our destiny and God's great promise. A day is coming when the whole universe will echo with the great hymn of praise; the great love-song of God. It is the song of every good desire—and the desire which lies beneath every good song. It is the song of all good things given and received. It is the song of godly suffering and human joy. It is the song of kindness and of courage and of the cross. It is the song of repentance and redemption, of righteousness and of resurrected life.

Oh yes, we will sing. The shape of the melody has already been inscribed upon our hearts. Are we learning to enjoy the song? Are we learning to find our utmost joy in the pursuit of the Christ-shaped life?

Bibliography

Allender, Dan, and Tremper Longman. *Bold Love*. Colorado Springs, CO: NavPress, 1992.

Bonhoeffer, Dietrich. *The Cost of Discipleship*. New York: Simon & Schuster, 1995.

Briones, David E. "Why Can't We Be Friends? Paul and Aristotle on Friendship." In *Paul and the Giants of Philosophy: Reading the Apostle in Greco-Roman Context*, edited by Joseph R. Dodson and David E. Briones, 36–49. Downers Grove, IL: Intervarsity, 2019.

Brunner, Emil. *The Great Invitation and Other Sermons*. Philadelphia: Westminster, 1955.

Carpenter, Micah D. *A Scandalous People: Ephesians on the Meaning of Christian Faith and Human Life*. Eugene, OR: Wipf & Stock, 2020.

Gorman, Michael. *Inhabiting the Cruciform God: Kenosis, Justification, and Theosis in Paul's Narrative Theology*. Grand Rapids, MI: Eerdmans, 2009.

Middleton, J. Richard. *A New Heaven and a New Earth: Reclaiming Biblical Eschatology*. Grand Rapids, MI: Baker, 2014.

Olson, Roger. "A Test of the Authenticity of Your Christianity." *Roger E. Olson* (blog), September 24, 2020. https://www.patheos.com/blogs/rogereolson/2020/09/a-test-of-the-authenticity-of-your-christianity.

Plato. *Phaedo*. In *The Last Days of Socrates*, translated by Hugh Tredennick, 111–12. New York: Penguin, 1969.

Willard, Dallas. *The Divine Conspiracy: Rediscovering Our Hidden Life in God*. San Francisco: HarperCollins, 1998.